WOODFIELD COOKS

WOODFIELD COOKS

A Community Collection edited by
ANN McCOLL LINDSAY
HAZEL DESBARATS
ULLA TROUGHTON

Illustrations by
DAVID LINDSAY

Proceeds from the sale of this book will help to keep the
Woodfield Community Green and Residential to the Core.

Copyright © 2010 The Woodfield Community Association

All rights reserved. No part of this book may be reproduced in any form or by any means, electronic or mechanical, including information storage and retrieval systems, without permission in writing from the publisher, except by a reviewer who may quote brief passages in a review.

Library and Archives Canada Cataloguing in Publication

CIP data on file with the National Library and Archives

ISBN 978-1-926582-49-8

www.historicwoodfield.com

Foreword
From Roast Pig to Tofu

The Cook Not Mad, 1831, has the distinction of being the first cook book to be published in Canada. The author provides us with this recipe for stuffing a pig that is to be roasted or baked:

> *Boil the innards tender, mince fine, add half loaf bread, half pound butter, four eggs, salt, pepper, sweet marjoram, sage, summer savory, thyme, mix the whole well together; stuff and sew up; if the pig be large let it be doing two and a half hours; baste with salt and water.*

At the time this was written, Colonel Thomas Talbot was hewing an extensive kingdom out of the woods and supervising agrarian land settlement in our area. A brass plaque on the lawn of Lord Roberts School in the heart of Woodfield, records that this Lake Erie Baron died where the school now stands in our community. The foods he grew and animals he raised are once more in vogue. Today's latest cook books are all about growing your own, eating fresh and local. In many Woodfield gardens you can find the herbs listed in the above recipe.

We even stuffed a pig and roasted it at our first Summerfests. Carling Heights Community Gardens, on our doorstep, provides plots for many of our families to grow their own vegetables.

When the Colonel was invited to Eldon House for Christmas, he helped Mrs. Harris pluck the wild goose her husband had shot for dinner. In this collection, Ulla Troughton presents a complete Christmas dinner with roast goose and all the trimmings.

Talbot advised immigrants to bring seed for potatoes and corn to plant before clearing the fields for other grain. The corn was ground by hand for meal. Our submitters have sent in recipes for corn bread, corn chowder, several for roasted potatoes, potato soup, as well as one for potato pie.

One of Talbot's chief delights was to take his canoe into the local creeks to catch fish that he prepared over an open fireplace. Rod McDowell has given us his recipe for baked trout, still available fresh from a fish farmer in our local market.

As his fiefdom on the cliffs of Lake Erie prospered, he served his guests duck and chicken from his poultry yard, lamb and beef from his pastures. I doubt that even the Colonel could have prepared a better steak and kidney pie than our own Hazel Desbarats. An orchard with apple, pear, plum and cherry trees provided desserts, not unlike the fruit tarts and puddings in our dessert chapter.

These culinary roots have been enriched by exposure to global ingredients. Recipes from over twenty countries reflect our international tastes. The brief introductions at the beginning of the recipes will give you a sense of the broad spectrum of people who cook in this residential core tucked behind City Hall. You'll find out what inspires them and how what they eat reflects how they live. *Woodfield Cooks* is a culinary/cultural snapshot of a community.

ANN McCOLL LINDSAY

Introduction

This collection differs from other 'charity' cookbooks in several respects. Rather than squeezing five cryptic recipes on a page, most of our recipes have been given a page or more to allow for a contributor introduction and detailed instuctions.

Where appropriate, an illustration of a kitchen utensil, drawn by David Lindsay, accompanies the recipe. After others, a space is provided for you to add comments or seasonal variations. Annotations of personal preferences allow you to become part of the creative cooking process.

Thanks to archivist, Glen Curnoe, we include a sprinkling of heirloom recipes from earlier collections, compiled by local retailers, industrialists, and church groups, affiliated with this community. These historic cookbooks tell us much about the families who lived here over fifty years ago.

The editors have diligently acknowledged source material and will endeavour to correct omissions or errors in future printings.

Our *Local Suppliers* list is a compilation of submitters' shopping recommendations. This is not a paid advertisers list. They have earned our support by carrying good products. We hope these suggestions help you to find special ingredients close to home. Hug a Farmer.

A Metric Conversion Chart is included to help you determine amounts required when buying packaged products.

In addition to the standard chapter groupings found in most cookbooks, we have added one called *Seasonal Celebrations*. Much of our best cooking is on show at events involving the community - Plant Exchange; Lawn Sale; Harvestfest; Christmas Carolling; the New Year. These traditional gatherings have become annual rites of passage.

We decided to dedicate the final chapter to the youth in our community. Two young professional Woodfield dieticians have suggested a typical daily menu to establish basic good food habits. The chapter ends with Nan Finlayson, retired kindergarden teacher at Lord

Roberts School, inviting us to sit in on cooking classes for five-year-olds. A positive note for the future of our community.

Table of Contents

Foreword		5
Introduction		7

Appetizers

French Chicken Liver Pâté	Emma Squire	17
Marinated Eggplant	Bob Bozak	19
Coeur au Chèvre Frais	Hilary Moon	21
Pimentos in Vinaigrette	Christine Troughton	23
Sangria	Hilary Moon	25
Gravad Lax	Linda Bussière	27
Eggs Romanoff	Judy Hately	30
Spanakopita Muffins	Bonnie Whitaker	32
Quiche Tartlets	Joan Clayton	34
Roasted Red Pepper Hummus	Jennifer Prgesa	36

Salads

Kurdish Salad	Judy Elliott	39
Coronation Chicken	Ann Fiske	40
Katherine Margaret's Lentil Salad	Angie Killoran	42
Salad Niçoise	Hazel Desbarats	43
Grain Salad Bar	Wanda Sawicki	44
	Lorraine de Blois	
Quinoa Salad	Christine Troughton	46
Watercress Salad	Ben Sterk	48

Soups

Bob's Corn Chowder	Bob Bozak	51
Carrot Orange Ginger	Ann Lindsay	53
Comfort Soup	Lorraine de Blois	55
Apple Soup	Judy Bryant	57
Parsnip/Pear	Michael Harkins	59

French Canadian Pea Soup	Anglican Church Women, Bishop Cronyn Memorial Church	60
Beef Barley	Emily Breau	62
Lentil Soup	Peggy Curnoe	63
Beef Goulash	Michael Harkins	64
Chicken/Noodle Comfort Soup	Lavarre Clark Dundas St. United Church	66
Gazpacho Evolution	John Thorp	69
	Michael Harkins	70
	Ann MacKenzie	72
	Marty Robinson	

Vegetarian Main Courses

Ratatouille	David Lindsay	77
Cauliflower and Lentil Curry	Hazel Desbarats	79
Zucchini Gratin	Lorraine de Blois	81
Asparastrata	Judith Warren	83
Potato Pie	Joey McDowell	85
Green Tomato Pie	Jane Bigelow	87
Spanakopita	Linda Bussière	89
Baked Beans	Peggy Curnoe	92
Lentils alla Turca	Regina Moorcroft	94
Tom's Jalapenos Rellenos	Tom Benner	95

Pasta

Pasta with Lobster and Chilies	Josie Squire	101
Swiss Chard Lasagna	Christine Troughton	105
Pasta con Piselli	Rod McDowell	107
Spaghetti Bolognese	Rod McDowell	109
Sarah's Spaghetti Sauce	Elizabeth Waterston	111
Pasta with Tuna and Olives	John Thorp	113
Co-op Pasta	Barbara Jones Warwick	115
Hot Penne Pasta	Kate Rapson and Jeff Carson	118
Hot Pasta/Cold Sauce	Christine Troughton	120

Seafood

Steamed Fish	Haiyun Chen	123
Salmon with Secret Dill Sauce	Francine Lacroix	125
	Queen's Village for Seniors	
Annie's Sole	Annie McColl	127
Comfy Fish Pie	Benedict Lockwood	128
Peter Desbarats' Shrimp Dish	Peter Desbarats	130
Curried Fish Dish	Ulla Troughton	132
Grilled Salmon	Catherine Mallory	133
Baked Trout	Rod McDowell	135
Fish and Chips	Ruth Hoch	137

Principal Plates

Leberli mit Rosti	Benedict Lockwood	141
Adobo Chicken	Melissa Briones	144
Braised Lamb Shanks	Mickey Apthorp	146
Tarragon Rice with Chicken Curry	Janet Dauphinee	149
Mild Chicken Curry	Hilary Moon	151
Curried Vegetables with Your Choice of Protein	Millie Hearn	153
Piccata of Pork	John Thorp	155
Giant Meatballs in Caper Sauce	Kathrin Campbell	157
Pad Thai	Christine Troughton	159
Steamed Ribs with Black Bean Sauce	Haiyun Chen	161
Glazed Spareribs	Peggy Curnoe	163
Indonesian Buffet	Irene Say	165
Rouladen	Regina Moorcroft	168
Boeuf Daube Niçoise avec Gnocchi	Ann Lindsay	169
Lamb Tajine aux Poires	John Thorp	172
Steak and Kidney Pie	Hazel Desbarats	174
Irish Beef Stew	Gabriele Sanio	177
A Steak by Any Other Name	Ruth Hoch	179
	Angie Killoran	
	John Thorp	

Sides and Sauces

Traditional Chinese Pancakes	Hong Chen-DeCloet	185
Roast Potatoes	Riva Ellinson	187
Curried Mayonnaise	Jim Cooke	189
Red Cabbage	Regina Moorcroft	190
Mushroom Loaf	Peggy Curnoe	192
Cumberland Sauce	Lorraine de Blois	193
Herb Rice	Kristen Gaudet	194
To Die for Mashed Potatoes	Kristen Gaudet	194
Homemade French Fries	Kristen Gaudet	195
Brilliant Broccoli	Benedict Lockwood	196
Maple Walnut Brussel Sprouts	John Thorp	197
Conserving Tomatoes	Ann Lindsay	198

Desserts

Mocha Torte	Alice Thomson	203
Chocolate Truffle Cake	Irene Say	205
Brandied Peach Butter	Kate Rapson	207
Peach Tart	Ann Lindsay	208
Versatile Pie Pastry	Ann Lindsay	210
The Bishop's Pudding	Dorey Jackson	212
Danish Fruit Pudding	Ulla Troughton	214
Spirited Fruit Crisps	Hazel Elmslie	216
Applesauce Cake Roll	P. Stone	218
Poppy Seed Cake	P. Stone	220
My Grandmother's Cheesecake	John Wegman	222
Sour Cream Pudding	Janice Lemieux	224
A Sweetheart Date Cake	Sweetheart Brand Cookbook	226
Ice Cream Memories	Ulla Troughton	228

Bread and Baked Goods

Hope Lodge Bagels	Dana Berman	233
Old Fashioned Gingerbread	How to Use Your McClary Range	235
Scottish Scones	Kim Harrison	237

Light Christmas Cake	Kate Rapson	239
Turtle Oat Squares	Helen Albert	241
Gentlemen's Chocolate Kisses	Smallman & Ingram's Cook Book	243
Corn Bread	Ruth Hoch	245
Lemon Bread	Anglican Church Women, Bishop Cronyn Memorial Church	247
Egg Tarts Freeport	Bonnie MacLachlan	248
Butter Tarts	Hazel Desbarats	250
Prince Albert Cake	Alice E. Boomer	251
Generations of Shortbread	Bonnie Whitaker	253

SEASONAL CELEBRATIONS

SPRING

Cranberry Muffins	Margaret Howe	259
Carrot Cake Muffins	Jennifer Prgesa	261
Salad of Herbs and Edible Flowers	The Garden Fairies	263

SUMMER

Roast Chicken	Ashleigh Barney	265
Margaritas	Rob Barney	268
Salad Caprese	Linda Whitney	270
Figs with Prosciutto	Mickey Apthorp	272

AUTUMN

Teriyaki Sweet and Sour Wings	Benedict and Helen Lockwood	274
Goodie's Roast Vegetables	Angie Killoran	276
Pear Tart	Ulla Troughton	278

WINTER

Squash Soup	Jennifer Prgesa	280
Glögg for Adults	Ulla Troughton	282
Banana Cake	Mrs. Clarence Peterson	284

Candied Christmas Tree	Santa's Elves	286
Chocolate Macaroons	Julia MacGregor	288
Mincemeat Fruitcake	Kim Harrison	290
Hot Spiced Cider	Hilary Moon	292
Roast Goose Dinner	Ulla Troughton	295
Christmas Mincemeat Tarts	Hazel Desbarats	298
Scottish Shortbread	Wes Kinghorn	301
New Year's Levée	Lorraine de Blois and Michael Robbins	303
Cassoulet	David Lindsay	304

A Healthy Future

Introduction to Healthier Eating Habits	Melissa Briones and Kristen Gaudet	309
Homemade Granola	Kristen Gaudet	310
Banana Pancakes	Kristen Gaudet	312
Alicia's Maple Smoothie	Alicia Wilkins	314
Additional Smoothie Combination	Melissa Briones and Kristen Gaudet	315
Health-Smart Luncheon Suggestions	Melissa Briones	316
Andes Omelet	Melissa Briones	318
Tasty Supper Tips	Melissa Briones	320
Fresh Salsa	Melissa Briones	322
Carrot Yogurt Dip	Regina Moorcroft	324
Squash-Cheese Dip	Kristen Gaudet	325
Banana Chocolate Chip Muffins	Kristen Gaudet	327
Applesauce	Nan Finlayson	329
Cranberry Relish	and Lord Roberts	
Sushi Sandwiches	Students	331

APPETIZERS

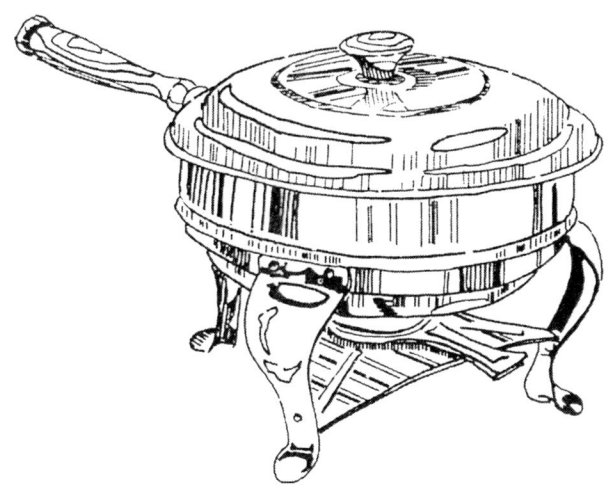

Creamy French Pâté

My sister Josie and I have spent all of our childhood living in and around Woodfield. A lot of our memories revolve around food from the pig roasts at Lord Roberts to hours spent in the kitchen of the Auberge de Petit Prince watching our dad cook. Now as adults we have returned to build our own families here in our favourite neighbourhood. We have submitted a couple of recipes from our Dad's Secret Files that have remained our favourites.

No holiday can go by without a yummy bowl of Chicken Liver Pâté served with those little sour pickles and grainy mustard.

Ingredients
1/4 cup unsalted butter
1/2 cup onions, diced
1/2 cup apple, diced

1/4 cup butter
1 pound chicken livers
1 bay leaf
1 teaspoon salt
1/2 teaspoon pepper
1/2 teaspoon thyme
1/2 teaspoon marjoram

1 ounce heavy cream
1/4 cup butter
1/4 to 1/2 tablespoon brandy

Method
1. Melt the butter in a sauté pan.
2. Cook the diced onions and apples together until tender but not browned.

3. In a separate pan, cook the second group of ingredients until livers are just done.
4. Combine onion/apple mixture and liver mixture.
5. Place them in a food processor with the remaining ingredients.
6. Whirl until smooth.
7. Pack into a small covered pâté terrine.
8. Allow to mellow a few hours or overnight in the refrigerator.
9. Serve with thin slices of baguette or brown toast triangles.

EMMA SQUIRE

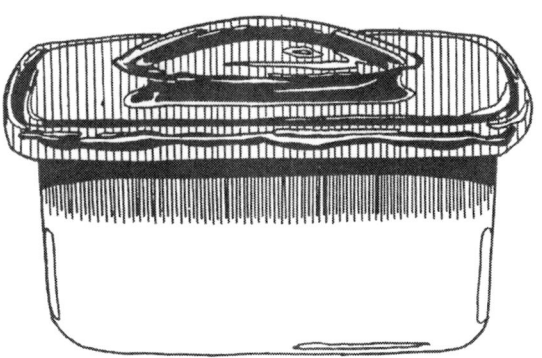

Marinated Eggplant

Bob Bozak was one of the founding members of London's Co-op Food Store. Their first load of produce was sorted and bagged on Bob's porch. He is an artist and the skilled potter who made the handsome coffee mugs used by HasBeans in the Market to serve cappucino to customers who ask for it in a mug.

He has been making this recipe for about twenty years. It was adapted from an Italian recipe and has been served to many people with great appreciation, getting positive reviews from guests who are not fond of eggplant.

Ingredients

2 large or 4 medium sized eggplants (Sicilian are very nice)
coarse salt
1 cup fresh basil leaves
2 large cloves garlic
vegetable oil (I use safflower, canola would do, but olive oil solidifies in the fridge)
freshly ground pepper
1/3 to 1/2 cup good quality balsamic vinegar (the better the quality, the better the taste)

Method

1. Slice the unpeeled eggplant into 1/2 inch rounds and place the slices on a large cookie sheet, overlapping slightly so there is an incline for the shedding liquid.
2. Sprinkle sparingly with coarse salt and let stand for an hour or more.
3. Scrape off the eggplant liquid and remaining salt. There will be a little salt remaining but that is fine. It eliminates the need to salt later.
4. Dry the eggplant slices with paper towels and fry them in large

quantities of oil until golden brown on both sides. The eggplant will absorb considerable oil so add as needed.
5. Place undrained slices on a platter and allow to cool.
6. During the frying process, chop the basil leaves and place them in a small bowl.
7. Chop the garlic finely, add to the basil and mix well with a wooden spoon.
8. Place a layer of eggplant in a serving dish or shallow casserole, cover with some of the chopped basil and garlic and then add ground pepper.
9. Set aside some of the garlic and basil mix for the top layer and continue layering until all of the eggplant and garlic/basil mix has been used.
10. Pour the balsamic vinegar on top, cover the dish with tin foil and place in the fridge.

    After an hour, tip the dish and turn so that the oil and vinegar mixes and moves around over the eggplant. Alternatively, tip and spoon.
11. Repeat several times over a few hours.

This dish is better when made the day before. The marinated eggplant will keep well in the fridge for several weeks and even longer if placed in a jar and covered with olive oil.

Serve on a fresh crusty baguette to at least 6 to 8 lucky people.

BOB BOZAK

Coeur au Chèvre Frais

Hilary Moon owned and operated the legendary Say Cheese, restaurant, bakeshop and cheese emporium for a total of twenty-eight years in London's core commercial district.

This lovely summer dish Ruth Klahsen and Hilary dreamed up one June for the Seasonal Menu at Say Cheese. They served it with a small watercress or tomato and fennel salad - use your imagination in serving this - smoked salmon is a natural.

Fresh herbs can be chopped and folded in with the cheese, but somehow the plain Coeur and other ingredients added on the side, seem to be the most delicious way to make it. You might put a sprig of fresh thyme, or a couple of basil leaves on the dampened cheese cloth before spooning the cheese mixture in and when turned out the herbs are imprinted into the top of the cheese.

Equipment
Six individual coeur à la crème perforated heart moulds or one large heart-shaped mould. (see supplier list) It is possible to buy tin gelatin or cake moulds and pierce them with nails for the drainage. Just make sure you dry thoroughly to prevent rusting.

You need enough cheese cloth to line the moulds and fold over the top.

Ingredients
- 8 oz fresh, uncured, goat milk cheese (chèvre frais) or 8 oz quark (fresh cream cheese)
- 4 egg whites
- 1/4 teaspoon salt
- 1/2 cup cream (as rich as you like it)
- Fresh herbs to decorate
- Home-made tomato salsa (or chilled ratatouille)

Method

1. Beat egg whites until stiff
2. In another bowl combine the first 4 ingredients (except the fresh herbs and salsa) and mix well.
3. Fold in the egg whites gently, one third at a time.
4. Line moulds with dampened cheese cloth and fill to top with cheese mixture, spooning it in gently so as not to make it heavy.
5. Fold the extra cheese cloth over the top of the mixture to cover the top completely.
6. Place the moulds on individual saucers or a plate that is deep enough to catch the whey which will drain out as the mixture thickens .
7. Cover the moulds with Saran wrap.
8. Allow to drain 6 to 8 hours or overnight in the refrigerator.
9. Just before serving, peel back the cheese cloth covering. Place serving plate over the top of the coeur mould and turn upside-down onto plate.
10. Decorate with fresh herb sprigs.
11. Spoon over the tomato salsa and serve with hot buttered toast, or crusty French bread.

Hilary Moon

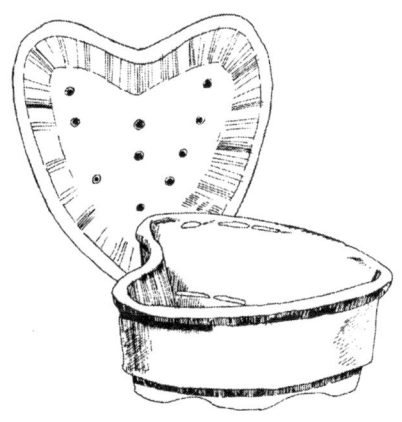

Pimentos in Vinaigrette

Christine Troughton is on the board of directors of Heart-Links, a London-based charitable, not-for-profit organization which has worked for the past 15 years to support through friendship and funding several impoverished and vulnerable communities in northern Peru. Programs are operated totally on a volunteer basis and include three comedores (community kitchens) which not only feed the most at risk children in the community, but are also vehicles for providing skills and practical experience to the women who run them.

These pimentos were a big hit when served by Christine on a tapas table at a summer neighbourhood gathering.

Ingredients
3 red peppers
1/2 teaspoon Spanish style paprika
1 tablespoon water
3 tablespoons olive oil
2 tablespoons red wine vinegar
salt and freshly ground pepper to taste
1/2 teaspoon thyme
1 clove garlic, sliced
1 teaspoon minced parsley
1 bay leaf
1 tablespoon slivered onion.

Method
1. Preheat oven to 375F.
2. Roast the peppers 15 to 18 minutes each side.
3. Core, seed and cut into half inch wide strips.
4. In small bowl dissolve paprika in the water. Whisk in oil, vinegar, salt, pepper and thyme.

5. Stir in the garlic, parsley, bay leaf and onion.
6. Add the pimento strips and marinate, refrigerated, until ready to use. They gain in flavour if left overnight.

A jug of Sangria makes an excellent accompaniment.

CHRISTINE TROUGHTON

Sangria

It seems that a traditional Sangria recipe is much forgotten since it has now become 'Americanized' and such things as 'Fresca' and 7Up are commonly thrown in. Well, we all need to be willing for change, but there's nothing quite like remembering that wonderful afternoon at a small table in a Spanish off-street square, enjoying a few olives, a gazpacho salad and a jug of colourful, refreshing Sangria - Spanish style! We've served it frequently here in Woodfield on our little back deck, and it always brings a romantic, rustic feeling to a summer afternoon.

Ingredients

2 bottles inexpensive, dry red wine - preferably Spanish or Portuguese
juice of 1 fresh large orange (or 2 small ones if they are juicier and sweeter)
1 tablespoons sugar
4 oz Brandy
1 orange, sliced
1 lemon thinly sliced
1 apple thinly sliced
1 peach cut in slices
1/2 bottle soda water
ice cubes

Method

1. Place the sliced peach, apple, lemon and orange into a bowl that has a fitting lid.
2. Add the sugar and the brandy, cover with the lid and allow to macerate at least for a couple of hours; I usually allow it to macerate at room temperature overnight.
3. Just before serving, put the macerated fruits and the orange juice into a jug, add the bottles of wine, ice cubes, and at the very last minute, the soda water.

4. Stir and pour into glasses decorated with slices of orange or lemon.

New Yorkers have added Triple Sec as an urban, sophisticated variation. I am a traditionalist, and enjoy the kick of brandy.

HILARY MOON

Hilary's friends partied with jugs of Sangria served with delicious tapas to celebrate a significant birthday in grand style.

Gravad Lax (cured salmon)

Our family lived in Uppsala, Sweden from 1992 to 1994 while my husband was a post-doctoral student at the university. Our oldest daughter Lucy was 1-1/2 years old when we moved there, and her brother Zach was born in Sweden a year later. We had the wonderful opportunity to return to Sweden for a year in 2007, so we rented out our house in Woodfield and set off for the land of strong coffee, dark winters and the long, long days of summer.

Our favourite memories of Sweden are times we ate delicious meals with friends, often outdoors in the long summer days in June, when the light still lingers well into the night. The table would be spread with the many dishes typical of a Swedish "smörgåsbord". There would be good conversation, and good food.

Gravad lax means literally "grave salmon". During the Middle Ages fisherman in Scandinavia would salt their salmon and ferment it by burying it in the sand up on shore. The gravad lax served these days is still cured with salt, but rather than fermented, it cures in the refrigerator.

To celebrate spring this year, and our return to Woodfield, we held a party in our back garden where we served gravad lax and the strongest coffee in the neighbourhood.

London is a good distance from the sea. Fortunately, it does have some good fish shops, like the one on Hamilton Road, run by a family of Portuguese descent.

Gravad lax is dry cured using sugar and dill, as well as salt. The prepared fish needs to cure for 1 or 2 days in the refrigerator, so give yourself a few days time when serving this dish.

Equipment

You'll need a 10″ x 14″ x 2″ baking dish. A light weight is needed to top the salmon as it cures. We use a one pound packet of dried beans.

INGREDIENTS

3 lbs. fresh salmon (ask the fish monger to remove the bones but not the skin; the middle part of the fish works best)
just under 1/2 cup salt (table salt is fine, use sea salt if you have it, coarse salt also works)
just under 1/2 cup sugar
2 tablespoons white peppercorns, crushed
fresh dill, a generous bunch or two

METHOD

1. If the salmon is whole, it will need to be filleted and bones removed. Keep the skin on. Use the thickest, middle part of the fish.
2. Mix the salt, sugar and crushed peppercorns.
3. Rub the salmon with about 1/2 of this mixture.
4. Line the bottom of the baking dish with dill, place half the salmon fillet skin down.
5. Cover with another layer of dill, and evenly sprinkle the rest of the salt/sugar/peppercorn mixture.
6. Place the second fillet, skin side up on top. Our booklet "A Small Treasury of Swedish Food", produced by the Federation of Swedish farmers in 1989 recommends placing the fillets opposite to how they were cut, thick end matching up to the narrow thin end.
7. Cover the skin side of the second fillet with another layer of dill.
8. Place a light weight on top of the fish. We use a 1 lb. packet of dried beans. Do not make it too heavy or the fish will lose all its juices. Refrigerate.
9. Turn the salmon over after 1 day curing. Keep refrigerated for second day.

TO SERVE

Scrape off the dill and peppercorns.
Slice the gravad lax thinly and arrange on a plate. Garnish the

plate with fresh dill and lemon wedges. The typical hovmästare sås can accompany the dish, though we've come to prefer the lax on its own.

Hovmästare Sås (cold mustard sauce)
2 tablespoons dry mustard
2 tablespoons sugar
2 tablespoons white vinegar
4 tablespoons olive oil
4 tablespoons sour cream
fresh dill, chopped

1. Mix the mustard, sugar and vinegar into a paste in a bowl.
2. Stir the oil in a bit at a time until thickened.
3. Add the sour cream, and some chopped dill.

My husband Brian is usually the one who takes on the preparation and careful thin slicing of the gravad lax. He also makes the mustard sauce that accompanies the dish. The rest of the family helps to make, or buy, the other dishes on the "smörgåsbord". The children run up the street to the Portuguese bakery for bread, we set out a few varieties of pickled herring, fresh beets, boiled potatoes served with dill, and a green salad. We might drink akvavit (aquavit), the grain alcohol sometimes called schnapps, which is distilled and flavoured with caraway, anise, fennel or coriander seeds. Then we make the Swedish toast — Skål!

Linda Bussière

Editor's Note
Linda would probably be playing a CD by one of her bands, *Buttonfly* or *Panic on Pluto*. We see her whizzing past our gate on her way to the Central Library where she works and we marvel at how she juggles all her roles.

Eggs Romanoff

This recipe originated from the Russian Romanoff family. I received it from a dear friend Margie Glue who studied in France at the Cordon Bleu Cooking School. She was a wonderful chef. It has always been a big favourite at my dinner parties.

Ingredients

4 hard boiled eggs
3/4 cup mayonnaise
salt and pepper to taste
8 pumpernickel bread rounds or blini (small whole wheat Russian pancakes)
1/2 cup sour cream
1 oz caviar (inexpensive red or black lumpfish is readily available)
8 oz. smoked salmon
1-1/2 teaspoons of lemon juice
Watercress sprigs

Method

1. Peel and cut eggs in half
2. Mix the egg yolks with 1/2 cup of mayonnaise and salt and pepper
3. Fill egg whites with the above mixture
4. Place smoked salmon on top of each piece of pumpernickel bread or blinis
5. Place eggs (round side up) on top of salmon
6. Mix remaining mayonnaise with sour cream and lemon juice
7. Spoon sauce over eggs to coat them completely
8. Spoon caviar on top of eggs
9. Garnish entire plate with watercress

Serves 8

Judy Hateley

Company Tartlets

As you read the introductory sentences at the beginning of most of the recipes in this collection, it will become evident that Woodfielders have many interests, both in their work and in their leisure time. None of this interferes with partying. It is fitting that this first chapter contains two recipes adapted from main course versions to become fillings for the hors d'oeuvre platter.

Spanakopita Muffins (Spanakopitakia)

In Greece, Spanakopita is usually eaten as a snack food, at room temperature or even cold. The bite-sized shapes are call "spanakopitakia" (little spinach pies).

This shape is an alternative to the traditional triangular or square serving. The recipe comes from my daughter, Meredith Jones, who lived her formative years in the large turreted house on the corner of Prospect and Dufferin.

Equipment
large muffin tins if serving as a light lunch with salad
small tart-size tins if passing as hors d'oeuvres

Ingredients
8 cups of fresh spinach
3 eggs
5 tablespoons of chopped red or green onion
olive oil
1/2 cup melted butter
1 cup crumbled feta cheese or chèvre
4 tablespoons chopped fresh dill
a package of phyllo (fillo) pastry
salt and pepper to taste

Method

1. Preheat oven to 350F.
2. Steam spinach 2 or 3 minutes. Drain and chop.
3. Sauté onion for a few minutes in a teaspoon of oil.
4. Beat eggs. Add cooked onion, cheese and spinach.
5. Add dill, salt and pepper and mix well.
6. Cut 6 sheets of phyllo pastry in half.
7. Keep covered with a damp towel while you assemble to prevent it from drying out.
8. Brush each half with melted butter.
9. Fold in half and place in a muffin tin.
10. Fill with egg mixture and fold the edges over.
11. Brush top with melted butter.
12. Cook for 25 to 30 minutes at 350F.

Makes 12 large muffins or 24 small

Bonnie Whitaker

When Bonnie isn't painting the porch or hanging a new screen door on her Prospect Avenue home, she is running or cycling as she prepares for the next triathalon.

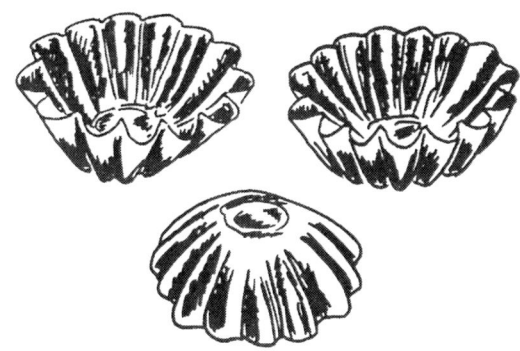

Quiche Tartlets

As a practising psychologist and a playwright, Dr. Joan P. Clayton combines the sciences with the arts. When she was 19, a friend passed on to her a unique recipe for quiche, which she had persuaded a chef at a small restaurant in Germany to part with. Joan has served it as a main course with a green salad to her family for years. The original quantities made two quiches (chefs cook for crowds). We have halved the ingredients to fill 30 tiny phyllo shells. It is a rich mixture which we think is at its best served in small tart shells as an appetizer at a party. This also allows you to try a variety of Joan's sugested toppings.

Ingredients
1 small sweet onion, or half a large one
2 tablespoons butter
8 ounces Swiss cheese
1 cup of sour cream
1 teaspoon corn starch
1/2 teaspoon baking powder
2 eggs
mini phyllo (fillo) shells or small pastry tarts

Joan's sugested toppings:
halved cherry tomatoes
broccoli flowerettes
slices of mushroom
asparagus tips
small squares of peppers
diced cooked ham

Method
1. Heat oven to 350F.
2. Finely chop the onion and sauté in butter.

3. Whisk the eggs and beat into the sour cream.
4. Stir in the corn starch and baking powder.
5. Grate the cheese. Fold it into the mixture.
6. Pour into partially baked pastry tart forms or mini fillo shells. (available in packages of 15)
7. Bake until custard is set. (approximately 20 minutes)
8. Steam your choice of garnishes. Mushroom slices and pepper pieces should be lightly sautéed in butter.
9. Top each mini tart with a garnish.

Makes 30 tartlets. Serve with a chilled New Zealand Oyster Bay Sauvignon.

DR. JOAN P. CLAYTON

Roasted Red Pepper Hummus

This recipe is a staple at all gatherings at my house. I work downtown and I moved to Woodfield so that I could walk to work in the morning. Soon the path became old hat and I started to read the newspaper on my way to work. I saw a recipe in the London Free Press several years ago for a dip called hummus that I had never heard of before. It was a recipe I believe by Jill Wilcox but I'm not sure and I no longer have the original.

We have checked with Jill who says she has printed several variations of hummus recipes and is pleased to have inspired this one.

Equipment
Food processor, latex gloves for handling peppers

Ingredients
1 19 oz can of chick peas drained or 2 cups of cooked chickpeas
1/4 cup tahini (sesame seed paste)
1/4 cup lemon juice
2 roasted red peppers (skins and seeds removed)
1 jalapeno pepper (wear disposable rubber gloves if removing the seeds) If you prefer hotter flavours, leave seeds in.
2 tablespoons olive oil
2 tablespoons water
1 clove garlic
1 tsp ground cumin

Method
1. Put all ingredients into a food processor except oil. Drizzle oil while pulsing to desired smoothness.
2. Serve with a basket of pita pockets.

Jennifer Prgesa

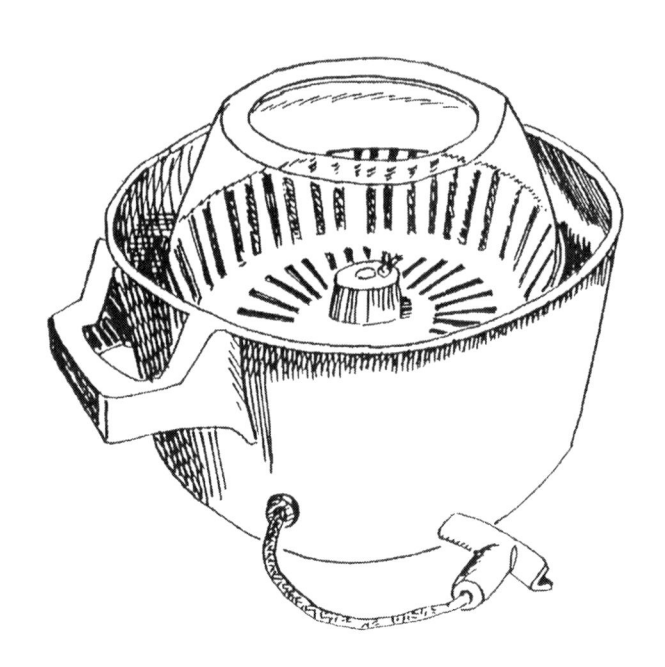

SALADS

Kurdish Salad

Several years ago I had a Kurdish English as a Second Language student in my house. He made this salad every night and sang along with a tape of Kurdish rebel songs while eating it. After all the salad was eaten he insisted that we share the remaining liquid, "good for health". It actually is refreshing.

Ingredients
For the salad:
1/4 English cucumber (1/2 cup)
2 medium to large tomatoes (1 cup)
1/4 large green pepper (1/2 cup)
1 green onion (1/4 cup)
3 cups of Romaine lettuce and leaf lettuce mixed

For the dressing:
juice of 1/2 large lemon (3 tablespoons)
3 tablespoons olive oil
2/3 teaspoon salt

Method
1. Whisk the dressing ingredients in the bottom of the salad bowl.
2. Peel the cucumber and chop it into small pieces.
3. Chop the tomatoes, pepper, and onion into small pieces.
4. Toss these vegetables in the dressing.
5. Set it aside at room temperature for at least 20 minutes. This allows the salt to draw some of the juice from the vegetables.
6. Break the lettuces into small pieces.
7. Toss the greens with the other vegetables immediately before use or the lettuce will wilt.

Every time I make this salad, I see the smiling face of my Kurdish student urging us to drink the remaining juice, "Full of what is good for you."

Judy Elliott

Coronation Chicken Salad

Ann and Harold Fiske live on the western edge of Woodfield overlooking Victoria Park and Ann has sent us a recipe fit for a queen. That's a fact – the dish was created for Queen Elizabeth's Coronation in 1953 by Constance Spry, a well known food writer in the UK. As an added bonus she also arranged the flowers. She was very talented. The recipe was subsequently included in "The Constance Spry Cookery Book", published in 1956. "Woodfield Cooks" has been given the royal thumbs up!

Ingredients

5 lbs chicken breasts
1 tablespoon vegetable oil
1 small onion, chopped
1 tablespoon curry paste or 1 teaspoon mild curry powder
1 tablespoon tomato purée (optional)
1/2 cup red wine
1 bay leaf
juice of 1 lemon
4 chopped apricot halves, fresh are best, canned will work
1 cup mayonnaise
1/2 cup plain or Balkan style yogurt
salt and pepper if desired
watercress to garnish

Method

1. Poach chicken breasts.
2. Cut into small, bite sized pieces.
3. In a saucepan, heat the oil. Add the onion and cook for about 3 minutes. Add the curry, tomato purée, wine, bay leaf and lemon juice. Simmer for about 10 minutes until reduced.
4. Cool.
5. Add the apricot pieces.

6. Add the mayonnaise and yogurt.
7. Mix in seasonings and then the chicken.
8. Add more lemon juice if desired.
9. Garnish and serve either as a salad or as a main course with boiled or roasted potatoes.

As a variation, crisp apple slices and celery may be substituted for the apricots.

Serves 8

ANN FISKE

Katherine Margaret's Lentil Salad

My sister-in-law deserves the credit for this recipe that our families have enjoyed for nearly 30 years. It was often on the menu for family dinners at our Bayfield cottage and was enjoyed by everyone from grandparents to toddlers. I use fresh basil and curly leaf parsley from my garden. The salad is easy to make and can be doubled or tripled to serve a crowd.

Ingredients

- 1-1/2 cups of green lentils (rinse in a strainer and discard any spoiled lentils)
- 1 28 oz can of local organic plum tomatoes
- 4 or 5 cloves of garlic peeled
- 3/4 cup chopped onion
- 1 cup of olive oil (sounds like a lot but it works)
- 1-1/2 cups of water
- bunch of fresh parsley chopped and stems removed (stems can be tied in cheesecloth and removed when cooked)
- 1 cup of coarsely chopped basil leaves
- 1 lemon

Method

1. Simmer all of the ingredients in large heavy pot partially covered for 1 to 2 hours until lentils are tender.
2. To serve, drain any excess liquid and scoop salad into a large bowl.
3. Remove garlic cloves, add fresh ground pepper, a squirt of fresh squeezed lemon juice and some more chopped parsley as garnish.

Serves 8

Angie Killoran

Make this recipe your own

line the bowl with arugula
crumble feta cheese on top

Salad Niçoise

When Peter and I were in Boston many years ago we picked up a copy of the Boston Globe Cookbook – a compilation of readers' recipes. While there are many recipes for Salad Niçoise we found this one to be the best. We have added extra ingredients to suit our taste.

Ingredients

1/2 lb green beans trimmed
1/2 cup good quality olive oil
1/4 cup good quality red wine vinegar
1 teaspoon Dijon mustard
freshly ground pepper to taste
1 medium red onion thinly sliced
2 medium tomatoes cut into wedges
2 oz. pitted black olives (Niçoise if possible)
1 can (2 oz) anchovy fillets, drained and chopped finely
2 small cans Mediterranean tuna (see supplier list)
3 hard boiled eggs, quartered
1 tablespoon chopped fresh basil
4 or 5 small new redskin potatoes, boiled in their skins and halved and at room temperature.
Fresh green lettuce to line the serving bowl

Method

1. Wash green beans, cut in half if desired and cook in very small amount of water until tender but crisp.
2. Whisk oil, vinegar, mustard, salt and pepper and toss with beans. Chill.
3. Place lettuce in large serving bowl. Add tomatoes, egg wedges, olives, tuna, anchovies, onions, fresh basil, potato halves. Top with green beans in dressing.
4. Mix gently at table and serve.

Serves 4

Hazel Desbarats

A Grain Salad Bar

Several neighbours are enthusiastic about making healthy main salads with various grains. Here is an opportunity for you to exercise your culinary creativity. Choose three or four grains, two types of fruit, a sample of nuts and green herbs or vegetables. Toss them with our suggested dressings.

These ingredients appear in recipes submitted by Wanda Sawicki and Lorraine de Blois. Grain cooking times vary. Refer to package directions.

INGREDIENTS

grains:	fruits:	vegetables:	nuts:
wheatberries	dried cranberries	parsley	walnuts
rye grain	dried cherries	green onions	pecans
barley	currants	celery	cashews
brown rice	raisins	carrots	
red rice	mandarin or tangerine		
wild rice	apple		

Wanda's Multigrain Pilaf Extravaganza

Wanda is an art therapist and an artist. She is so enthusiastic about this mixture of great ingredients, that she had better explain it in her own words:

"This recipe is so versatile! The grain combos may be altered to your taste, with wider varieties, such as oat and quinoa added in, provided the amount of cooking water is twice the amount of grains. Hemp hearts make a fine, nutty addition sprinkled into the finished mix. Other fruits, such as pineapple and blueberries may be used. Beans with corn add protein and pizzaz and cooked beets add colour. Experiment!

This dish keeps in the fridge for days, and is tasty cold, at room temperature or heated. It can be frozen in freezer bags, flattened, then broken off as needed for individual servings. Great added to a tossed green salad, or as a side with poultry, fish or meat."

METHOD

1. Wash a mixture of one cup of chosen grains by stirring them in two or three batches of cold water until clear.
2. Bring 2 cups of water to a boil. Stir in the grains, reduce heat to a bare minimum. Cover and cook until they are puffed and fluffy (about 30 minutes).
3. If any water remains, remove the lid, stir the grains and allow the water to evaporate.
4. Stir in the dried fruit of choice, cover for 5 minutes and shut off heat. Remove the lid and allow to cool.
5. Add a selection of vegetables, fresh fruit and nuts.
6. Toss with some olive oil and a squeeze of lemon juice to taste.

WANDA SAWICKI

At her New Year's Day Levée, Lorraine de Blois' guests rave over her bowl of wheat berries, brown rice and barley which she combines with two fruits and four vegetables from the list. She prefers to dress it with a sweet/sour vinaigrette which contains sugar and grated red onion tossed with a white vinegar and light vegetable oil.

Jane Bigelow, the Mayor of London in the 1970's, informs us that she makes her favourite bulgar salad so often that her cookbook falls open at the page. Bulgar is traditionally mixed with lots of chopped parsley, garlic, oil, mint and lemon juice. Soft grains, such as bulgar and couscous, require only a 15 minute soak in hot water.

Quinoa Salad

This colourful salad has appeared on Christine Troughton's Woodfield deck at least two or three times each summer for many years as an accompaniment to grilled vegetables and/or meat, or open sandwiches with grilled Portobello mushrooms and other delicious fillings.

Ingredients
2 tablespoons fresh lemon juice
1/4 cup olive oil
2 tablespoons minced cilantro
salt
1 cup fresh or frozen corn, simmered until tender
1/2 cup cooking liquid reserved
1/4 cup quinoa, rinsed thoroughly
1/4 teaspoon cumin seeds
1/2 cup canned black beans, rinsed
1 medium tomato, cut into small dice
2 tablespoons minced red onion

Method

1. Mix lemon juice, olive oil and cilantro for the dresssing.
2. Add one half teaspoon salt and set aside.
3. Bring liquid from corn to a boil in a small saucepan. Add quinoa and cumin; cover and simmer until quinoa absorbs the liquid and is tender, about 10 minutes.
4. Transfer quinoa to a large non reactive bowl; cool slightly.
5. Add corn and remaining ingredients and the dressing; toss and combine.
6 . Chill. Taste test for seasonings.

Serves 4

Christine Troughton

Watercress Salad

In the years that Ben and Briony Sterk lived in their home on Wolfe Street, they rallied residents to form a community association, to start designating their heritage homes and to save landmarks from demolition. But people often leave us with more than good works. When they returned to their native Australia, they left their good friend, Ulla Troughton, with memories of shared meals, social gatherings, and recipes. Here is one she is passing along to us.

Ingredients
2 bunches of watercress
2 cloves of garlic, minced
1/4 teaspoon salt
1 tablespoon of Dijon mustard
1/2 cup olive oil
3 tablespoons wine vinegar
3/4 cup yogurt
1 teaspoon brown sugar

Method
1. Rinse watercress.
2. Cut off some of the lower stems and discard, then cut up the rest of the watercress.
3. In a small bowl, mix together garlic, salt, mustard, oil, wine vinegar.
4. In another bowl, mix together yogurt and brown sugar.
5. Finally shake it all together and pour over watercress.

Ben Sterk

Make this recipe your own.
Try thin slices of mushroom or apples on top of the watercress.
A sprinkling of pomegranate seeds adds colour.

SOUPS

Bob's Corn Chowder

Sara and I have been living on Dufferin Avenue in Woodfield since 2001 where I have converted a solid but neglected ceramic block double garage at the back of the property into a pottery and art studio incorporating heritage elements. At some point in the past the building had served as the home for Blue Ribbon Ice Cream. I am currently preparing to make two large dinner sets and in the new year will begin working on a new body of art work.

I have been interested in cooking since I was a child and I suppose it is not coincidental that I make objects that relate to food preparation and serving. This recipe was an invention that came out of a need to not waste food. At Sara's parents' cottage in the Gatineau this summer there were two fridges overflowing with summer produce. The corn, potatoes and leftover ham were the basis of this soup. The roasted red peppers came from another recipe and, puréed with half of the corn kernels, provided a tasty contrast to the chunkiness of the other ingredients.

Ingredients

kernels from 10 or more corn cobs
organic chicken broth to cover, approximately 4 cups
2 cups roasted red peppers (homemade or from a jar)
1 large onion finely chopped
2 to 3 celery stalks thinly sliced
2 to 3 cups finely diced potatoes
10 oz lean bacon, left over ham or quality deli ham
water to cover potatoes
salt and pepper to taste
2 cups 18% cream
1 cup chopped parsley

To Roast red peppers
1. Preheat oven to 425F.
2. Cut tops off peppers and halve them.
3. Rub a little oil on skins and place them skin side up on baking sheet.
4. Place baking sheet in upper part of oven and roast for 20 to 25 minutes until skins are wrinkly.
5. Remove from oven and place in brown paper or plastic bag for about 15 minutes to steam.
6. Remove from bag and peel off skins.

Method
1. In a 4 litre saucepan simmer corn kernels in chicken broth until just tender. If the corn is very fresh it will take 4 to 5 minutes.
2. In a food processor purée half of the simmered corn kernels with all the roasted red peppers and set both aside.
3. Sauté finely diced bacon in a frying pan for a few minutes over medium heat until fat is released.
4. Add onion and celery to pan and continue cooking until the bacon is cooked.
5. Transfer to a large saucepan and add the diced potatoes and simmer until tender.
6. Add the puréed corn and the remaining corn kernels and bring to a slow boil.
7. Turn off heat, season with salt and pepper, blend in the cream and add the parsley.

Serves 8 to 10

Bob Bozak

Carrot, Orange, Ginger Soup

Equipment

The grating disc on a food processor does a quick job of grating carrots. Pack only two sticks at a time so that you do not put too much pressure on the disc.

Ingredients

1 tablespoon butter
1 tablespoon oil
3 shallots or 1 medium onion
8 carrots approximately 7 inches long
4 cups chicken or vegetable stock or enough to cover
2/3 cup of freshly squeezed orange juice
grated zest from one orange
1 inch piece of root ginger
salt and pepper to taste

Method

1. Melt butter and oil together in a large, heavy soup pot.
2. Stir in the finely chopped shallot or onion.
3. Scrub or peel the carrots. Grate them in small batches in the processor or on a fine-holed hand grater.
4. Toss with the softened onions.
5. Peel and grate the root ginger. Add it to the pot.
6. Pour in the orange juice and the stock.
7. Simmer gently covered for 30 minutes.
8. Add salt and pepper to taste.
9. Garnish with grated orange zest.

Serves 8 people as a starter. May be blended if a smooth soup is preferred.

Ann Lindsay

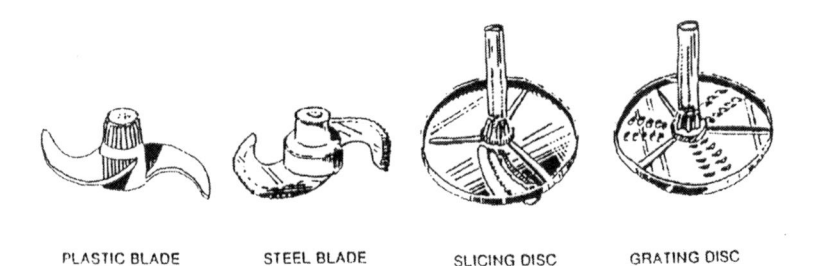

COMFORT SOUP

Lorraine de Blois clipped a recipe out of a newspaper fifteen years ago and lost it. She remembered the basics and used her cooking skills to innovate the rest of it. The result has since become a staple comfort dish in her home. With the amount of garlic involved it can also be relied upon to chase colds and vampires.

INGREDIENTS
2 garlic or farmers' sausages
2 tablespoons oil
1 large whole bulb of garlic, diced (6 to 8 cloves)
1 large leek diced
2 ribs of celery diced
2 to 3 medium potatoes diced
1/2 cup of white wine
4 to 5 cups of water
1/2 cup of parsley finely chopped
seasonings to taste

METHOD
1. Cook sausages in a heavy fry pan
2. In 4 quart soup pot, heat the oil and sauté until soft the garlic, leek and celery
3. Add potatoes, white wine and water to cover.
4. Simmer until the potatoes are cooked.
5. Add the parsley.
6. Cut the cooked sausage into small pieces.
7. Stir it into the soup.

Lorraine adds 2 teaspoons of her special salted herb mixture. It is a recipe from a Quebecois cookbook which instructs the gardener/cook to layer equal amounts of green herbs, chives, savoury, parsley, chervil, lovage, celery leaves, green onions, grated carrots, in a crock with a lesser amount of coarse salt sprinkled between the layers. After it is refrigerated for two weeks, you can spoon out small amounts to use in soups, stews and sauces. Just remember to squeeze out the moisture first and not to use additional salt in your recipe.

LORRAINE DE BLOIS

Apple Soup

Our Downtown Ward Councillor, Judy Bryant, is also an artist and theatrical costume designer. She grew up in New Zealand, graduated from the University of Toronto in Architecture and found her way to London's Historic Woodfield District. On her arrival in Canada in 1980 she says, "We hunted down recipes that reflected living in Ontario and I spotted this recipe in The Globe and Mail. It complemented Thanksgiving recipes we had gathered during our years in the USA. The variety of apples we use in the soup alters the flavour every time we make it. We recommend local apples from the Covent Garden Market where we enjoy shopping with fellow Woodfielders. This soup is always a hit with our neighbours."

Ingredients

6 apples, peeled cored and sliced
4 cups water
1 cup dry white wine
1/2 cup granulated sugar
grated rind of 1 lemon or orange
2 cups light cream (5%)
1/4 cup Calvados (apple brandy)
salt to taste
ground cinnamon to garnish

Method

1. In a saucepan simmer apples in water, wine, sugar and lemon rind until soft (15 to 20 minutes). Remove from heat and cool.
2. Blend apples and liquid to a purée in a blender, or food processor or with hand blender.
3. Return to heat and add cream, Calvados and salt.
4. Serve in heated bowls with a sprinkle of ground cinnamon.

This soup may also be served at room temperature. You can back off a little on the sugar and cream and substitute a little more water or Calvados if you find this too rich. But once in a while rich is nice! You can use a variety of apples but a sharp one like Granny Smith probably achieves the best result.

Serves 6

JUDY BRYANT

Parsnip and Pear Soup

Michael Harkins admits that he is a passionate cook. He particularly enjoys preparing dinners for his wife and three daughters. Here is one of his favourite soup recipes.

Ingredients

4 parsnips
2 carrots
3 pears
1 teaspoon ginger
4 or 5 cups stock (chicken or vegetable)

Method

1. Peel and dice the first three ingredients.
2. Place them in a soup pot with the stock and ginger.
3. Bring to a boil then simmer for an hour.
4. Purée with an electric hand blender or through a food mill. Add a little extra stock to desired thickness.

Serves 4

Michael Harkins

Make this recipe your own.

other root vegetables blend well with fruit:
celery root and potatoes
apples and squash

French Canadian Pea Soup

This soup is from a cookbook called "Father's Favourites", which was first printed in the 1950's. It was put together by the Anglican Church Women at Bishop Cronyn Memorial Church in Woodfield. The title refers to the priest at the time. It was a popular book and there was a second printing in 1983. Many bridal showers and Christmas stockings were blessed with this cookbook as a gift. The following recipe has been served many, many times at various lunches in the church through the years. Bishop Cronyn opens it's doors to street people on Tuesday mornings for coffee and they also volunteer a team of helpers to Dundas Street United Church for their "Out of the Cold" dinners offering both edible and spiritual comfort to anyone who comes in.

Ingredients

1 lb whole or split dried yellow peas
1/4 teaspoon baking soda
3 quarts cold water
1/2 lb. salt pork, or smoked pork hock, or ham bones.
1/2 cup carrots diced
1/2 cup turnip diced
1 chopped onion
salt and pepper to taste

Method

1. Soak yellow peas in cold water for 12 hours with baking soda.
2. Rinse well and cover with cold water . Add the salt pork or ham bones.
3. Bring to a boil, skim well, add diced carrots, turnips and onion.
4. Simmer 4 hours. Add salt and pepper to taste.
5. If desired, add savoury and parsley. Do not strain.

This is even better the second day. Serve with a tossed salad and crusty bread. We are grateful to Anne Henry, parish administrator, for bringing this collection to our attention

ANGLICAN CHURCH WOMEN, BISHOP CRONYN MEMORIAL CHURCH

Beef Barley Soup

Emily Breau lives in the Hayman Court Apartments. This recipe originated with her family in the British Isles and has been passed down for three generations. It makes nutritious use of beef left over from the Sunday roast.

Ingredients

2 cups of cooked beef cubed
1 cup of barley
1/2 cup of carrots
1/2 cup of onions
1/2 cup celery
1/2 cup mushrooms
1 cup of tomato juice
9 cups of beef broth (see supplier list for suggested bouillon)
chopped parsley for garnish
salt to taste

Method

1. Simmer the barley in the liquids for about a half hour while you dice the vegetables.
2. Add the cooked beef and root veg to the pot. Reserve the mushrooms.
3. Simmer for another hour.
4. Half the mushrooms if small or slice if large.
5. Simmer for another half hour, after adding mushrooms.
6. Serve with a sprinkling of parsley and some wholemeal bread.

Emily Breau

Lentil Soup

My mother often used to make this delicious soup for us. She always claimed that this recipe was given out by Pierre Berton when he was on Front Page Challenge.

Ingredients
2 cups lentils
6 cups water
4 single stalks of celery with tops attached
1 onion
4 carrots
1 clove garlic
1 28 oz can tomatoes
1/4 teaspoon oregano
1/4 teaspoon black pepper

Method
1. Rinse lentils well and discard any spoiled ones.
2. Peel and dice onion into small pieces.
3. Dice washed celery into small pieces including the green leafy tops.
4. Peel and dice carrots into small pieces.
5. Put all ingredients into large pot and bring to the boil, skim and reduce heat to simmer.
6. Cook for several hours until lentils are tender.
7. You can eat it as is, or put through a food processor for a completely smooth soup, or partially blend some for a chunkier texture.

Serves 6

Peggy Curnoe

Make this recipe your own
slices of a cooked hot, spicy sausage go well in this soup

Beef Goulash Soup

In central London, in a neighbourhood called Woodfield, two families live side by side. The Desbarats, Hazel, Peter and family, and the Harkins, Alex, Michael and family. Some years ago Peter was alone in the house one night – his wife, Hazel, was away acting in Edmonton – and he had a fall. His dogs, Teddy and Fergus were there to comfort him but were not much practical help. Anyway, Peter managed to call an ambulance to take him to hospital. When he awoke the next morning, neighbours Michael and Ulla Troughton were at his hospital bedside to make sure he was all right. The following week, recuperating at home, still alone, because as you know, in the theatre, the show must go on, Alex and Michael made sure he had a home-cooked dinner every evening. That is the spirit of neighbourliness in Woodfield. Since then the Desbarats have been the lucky recipients of some of Michael's creative cookery – like Beef Goulash Soup.

This recipe was first printed in the London Free Press in the 1980's and Michael had it many times for lunch at the Marienbad Restaurant. He has made some adaptations to the original recipe.

Ingredients

2 to 3 tablespoons vegetable oil
3 to 4 onions, peeled and sliced thinly
1/2 teaspoon caraway seeds (you can use more to taste)
1 lb stewing beef, trimmed of excess fat, and cut into cubes of 1/2 to 1 inch
1/3 cup tomato paste
1 tablespoon Spanish paprika
1/4 teaspoon cayenne, or to taste.
5 cups beef stock
2 potatoes, washed and diced (not necessary to peel them)
3 tablespoons flour for thickening
salt and pepper to taste.

Method

1. Heat the oil in soup pot until hot. Add the onions and caraway seeds. Reduce heat to medium low, and cook for about 5 minutes, stirring frequently.
2. Add the meat and brown over medium heat, stirring frequently, for 10 to 15 minutes.
3. Add tomato paste, spices and 3 cups of the stock. Simmer until meat is tender, for about an hour and a half, stirring occasionally.
4. Add the potatoes. Warm up the remaining stock and gradually whisk in the flour until there are no lumps. Add to the soup.
5. Simmer for 15 to 20 minutes or until the potatoes are cooked.
6. Season with salt and pepper to taste.

This soup can be kept in the fridge for a couple of days and freezes well. To stretch the recipe a little, use 2 lb meat, 1 tablespoon caraway seed, one 28 oz can of diced tomatoes with juice. You can use sweet potatoes instead of regular potatoes.

Michael Harkins

Chicken Noodle Soup

Food and fellowship are an integral part of church programmes and many churches in Woodfield are involved in some kind of hospitality outreach. In 1997 Dundas Street United Church recognized a growing need in the community and created their "Out of the Cold" dinners. Every Wednesday from mid-October until the end of May they serve a hot meal to anyone who walks through the doors of the Church. Seventy volunteers divided into four teams come in for the day to cook and serve the meal. The menus are varied and cut across the main food groups: hot soups, chili and pasta dishes, fresh vegetables and salads and, of course, desserts. Over 150 people usually turn up for a hot-cooked meal and in 2008 more than 4,300 dinners were served.

It seems highly appropriate that the ultimate comfort soup should be submitted by this group for our book. Originally designed for 30 people and served at many UCW lunches, this is our adapted version for a smaller group. We have chosen to start from scratch by simmering a chicken to make the stock - seems like a lot of work but the extra chicken can be used for other dishes, making it all worthwhile.

Ingredients
1 4 lb chicken
bunch of parsley including stalks
8 cups of stock from the cooked chicken
2 cups of the cooked chicken cut into bite sized pieces
2 teaspoons Dijon mustard
1 cup broken pasta (egg noodles or rice or linguini)
2 cups finely diced celery
1 large onion, finely diced
1 large carrot, finely diced
handful of chopped parsley
salt and pepper to taste

2 tablespoons vegetable oil or butter

Method
1. In large stock pot cover chicken with water and bring to boil. Simmer over low heat for about an hour and a half until chicken is tender.
2. Remove chicken and let cool. Wrap and store in refrigerator.
3. Let stock cool and place in refrigerator, preferably overnight.
4. The next day remove fat from surface of stock and reserve 8 cups of stock for the soup.
5. Remove meat from chicken and dice 2 cups and reserve. Discard skin and bones and keep remaining chicken for other dishes.
6. Heat oil over medium heat and sauté onion, carrot and celery for about 5 minutes or until onion is tender.
7. Add chicken stock and mustard and bring to boil, stirring occasionally.
8. Add chopped parsley to taste.
9. Break pasta into short lengths and simmer in the soup for about 8 minutes until tender.
10. Add cooked chicken and simmer a few minutes until hot.
11. Pour into good sized soup bowls and recover from whatever ails you.

Serves 10

Lavarre Clark, Dundas Street United Church

Make this recipe your own
"Woodfield Cooks" suggests using the leftover chicken for creamed chicken in vol-au-vents, one of the church's popular lunchtime entrees, and maybe a couple of chicken salad sandwiches as well. A pretty good amount of food from one chicken!

Jot down other uses for the cooked chicken.

The Gazpacho Evolution

The food introduced by an invading culture can have as much impact on a nation as a revolution. When the Muslim peoples crossed from North Africa to the south of Spain, they brought with them their preference for bread soaked in cold soup. The term gazpacho comes from the Arabic for soaked bread. In Roman and Greek literature, as well as the Bible, there are references to a type of drinkable food.

The Spanish contribution was their ability to keep the original dish light and fresh through centuries of hot summers. It is traditionally served as a thin purée of tomatoes, cucumbers, onions, green pepper, garlic, water, vinegar and olive oil. Bowls of chopped condiments are served separately for each diner to choose their garnish.

Canadian constitutions perhaps require a heavier interpretation. Our submitters prefer a chunky version of gazpacho.

John Thorp's Gazpacho

In its simplicity, this comes closest to the early Spanish tradition.

Ingredients
6 large ripe tomatoes
2 sweet red peppers
2 medium yellow onions
2 large shallots
2 large cucumbers
1/2 cup red wine vinegar
1/4 cup olive oil
1-1/2 cups canned tomato juice
pinch of cayenne pepper
salt and pepper
1/2 cup chopped fresh dill

Method
1. Chop all of the vegetables into fine dice.
2. Mix in a large glass jug or bowl with the liquid ingredients.
3. Chill well before serving.

John Thorp

Michael Harkins' Favourite Gazpacho

This is our family's favourite summer soup, when the field tomatoes and other vegetables are fresh, abundant and cheap. This recipe makes enough for our family of five twice over, but it is gone in less than two days. A couple of weeks last summer I made three batches. It is cool, tasty, refreshing and healthy. I started with a recipe from "The New Best Recipe Cookbook," working through three alterations until the four female tasters in the family reached agreement on the vegetable content and amount of seasonings. We prefer our soups chunky, but this one can be run through a blender. It is truly a liquid salad.

Ingredients

one half orange bell pepper, one half yellow, one half red and one half green
half a red onion
3 medium beefsteak tomatoes (about 12 ounces)
1 medium English cucumber
4 medium cloves of garlic
2 teaspoons salt
1 teaspoon pepper
one third cup red wine vinegar
6 cups of tomato juice
1 teaspoon Frank's hot sauce
1 tray of ice cubes

Method

1. Dice the tomatoes. You may discard the seeds if preferred.
2. Remove the white ribs and seeds from the peppers. Cut into fine cubes.
3. Chop red onion into fine pieces.
4. Peel the cucumber, seed and dice.
5. Finely mince the garlic.
6. Combine these vegetables with the remaining ingredients in a large bowl.
7. Cover tightly and refrigerate for a few hours.
8. Serve in a bowl - glass would be nice - or sip from a mug if the soup has been blended.

Michael Harkins

Herbal Gazpacho Soup

This recipe has been modified several times by us over the last thirty or so years. It is in our opinion the best recipe for gazpacho we have ever tried. The only drawback is that it is labour intensive but the food processor takes care of that problem. It differs from the others in the large variety of herbs included.

Ingredients

- 1 large red onion, peeled and quartered
- 2 fresh jalapeno chilies or medium hot canned green chilies
- 2 cloves garlic, peeled
- 4 large ripe tomatoes quartered, or a one pound can of Italian plum tomaoes
- 1 red bell pepper, seeded and quartered
- 1 large green bell pepper, seeded and quartered
- 1 regular cucumber, peeled and cut into large pieces
- 2 cups tomato juice, or 1 clamato juice and 1 tomato juice
- 1 cup tomato paste
- 2 long stalks celery cut into 1 inch pieces
- 2 green onions chopped, including the green part
- 1/2 lemon squeezed
- 1 teaspoon pimento (bottled)
- 2 tablespoons olive oil
- 3 tablespoons vinegar (wine or Balsamic)
- 1 teaspoon salt
- 1 teaspoon sugar
- 7 or 8 sprigs fresh cilantro
- 3 to 5 sprigs fresh tarragon
- 5 to 6 sprigs fresh thyme
- 5 to 6 sprigs fresh parsley
- several fresh basil leaves
- 3 to 5 sprigs oregano

Method

Process through the food processor until moderately smooth. If too thick add more tomato juice. Too sweet? Add a bit more vinegar. Not sweet enough? Add one half to 1 teaspoon sugar.

Garnish with slices of lime, or a sprig of basil. Serve chilled.

Serves 6 to 8

Marty Robinson and Ann MacKenzie

When the electric blender reached the Spanish shores, housewives embraced this machine, perfect for making their favourite soup. Now the food processor is changing the texture and number of ingredients in yet another twist in the Gazpacho story. To help your machine do a thorough job, we suggest that you process the first seven ingredients in small batches. Transfer them to your largest bowl along with the other hand cut vegetables, liquids and seasonings. If you want it smoother, feed it through the machine again two cups at a time.

VEGETARIAN MAIN COURSES

Ratatouille

David Lindsay's family grew up in country manses with large victory gardens. His home yard in Woodfield has been expropriated by his wife for flowers, so he is very grateful to have an allotment at the Carling Heights Community Gardens, just a few blocks away.

This recipe takes advantage of the fresh vegetables as they come in. Usually, the main ingredients, peppers, eggplant and zucchini are ready to be picked at the same time. Use a good quality olive oil as the vegetables absorb it for flavour. An orange or yellow pepper adds colour to this Provençal stew. A Spanish onion keeps the vegetable medley on the sweet side.

The past few summers, David has grilled the larger slices of vegetables before adding to the pan. It really enhances the flavours.

Ingredients
2 to 3 tablespoons olive oil
one large Spanish onion
one large red, yellow or orange pepper
two small or one medium eggplant
two small zucchini
two or three medium size tomatoes
two cloves garlic
10 fresh coriander seeds, salt and pepper

Method
1. Before cooking prepare the vegetables. Leave unpeeled and slice both the zucchini and eggplant into lengths or rounds. Lay the slices on paper towels and sprinkle lightly with salt. Leave for ten or fifteen minutes to allow the salt to draw out excess moisture. Repeat for the other side.
2. Core and cut the pepper into medium slices. Since this is a vegetable stew there is a certain amount of freedom in proportioning

and cutting. Coarse and thick cutting helps the vegetables retain their integrity while cooking.
3. Option: For added flavour, these vegetables can be further prepared by searing them with black marks for a few minutes in a grill pan or under a broiler.
4. Heat the olive oil in a heavy enamelled cast iron dutch oven over medium heat on the stove. Add the peeled, cut and sliced onion and sauté until lightly coloured, but not browned.
5. Add the pepper pieces and gently stir. After two or three minutes, add the sliced eggplant. Again, in a few minutes, add the sliced zucchini, crushed garlic and coriander seeds, pinch of salt and a few grinds of pepper. Stir gently, cover and cook at a simmer for fifteen minutes.
6. Remove the lid and add the tomatoes, coarsely chopped. Cover and cook gently for another ten minutes, stirring occasionally. Remove from heat and let sit until ready to serve. The cooking times and stirring should be watched so that each of the vegetables retains its shape and colour. Total cooking time approximately 30 to 40 minutes.
7. Garnish with chopped fresh parsley or basil. Can be served warm or cold.

DAVID LINDSAY

Cauliflower and Lentil Curry

This was one of the first recipes in my collection, dating back to when I first came to Canada in the early 1960's. I don't think I had ever tasted curry before. In England at that time it was not a popular dish. Now, of course, curry is the number one take-out in the U.K. This dish was made by a friend of mine who introduced me to the world of curries and it has continued to be a favourite over the years.

Ingredients
1 medium sized cauliflower
2 oz coconut oil (or butter)
1 cup red or yellow lentils
2 medium cooking onions, finely chopped
1/2 teaspoon ground chili
1/2 teaspoon ground turmeric
1 rounded teaspoon mild curry paste, or more to taste (curry powder can also be used)
3 tablespoons unsweetened dessicated coconut
1 cup water
juice of half a lemon

Method
1. Rinse cauliflower and break into small florets, discarding most of the stems. Set aside in colander.
2. Rinse lentils, place in saucepan with 3 cups of water bring to boil and simmer, covered, for 15 minutes until soft. They go fairly mushy.
3. While lentils are cooking, heat coconut oil in saucepan, preferably enamelled iron pot and sauté onions for 4 to 5 minutes until soft but not brown.
4. Add spices and cook over low heat for several minutes.
5. Add cauliflower, lentils, coconut and a good pinch of salt.

6. Pour in 1 cup of water and cook on low heat until cauliflower is tender 15 to 20 minutes. Serve on a bed of cooked basmati rice with a squirt of lemon juice.

Fruit chutney, toasted almonds, raisins dollop of plain yogurt, poppadums or chapatis are all nice accompaniments. You can vary the amount of curry paste, or powder to suit your own taste but it is not meant to be a fiery dish.

Serves 6

HAZEL DESBARATS

Zucchini Gratin

This is Lorraine de Blois' variation of a popular Italian classic. It answers her personal need to put her baskets of garden produce to good use.

Equipment
a 9 inch by 12 inch baking pan or earthenware au gratin

Ingredients
2 cups of tomato sauce (prepared)
or if making from scratch:
1 tablespoon olive oil
1 clove of minced garlic
1 medium onion diced
2 cups of garden tomatoes or canned Italian plum tomatoes, puréed with the juice
1 bay leaf
1 tablespoon fresh basil or 1/2 tablespoon dried
1/2 teaspoon salt
a few grinds of fresh pepper

4 medium zucchini
1 tablespoon of oil
1 clove of garlic

2 tablespoons finely ground bread crumbs (preferably from firmly textured bread)
2 tablespoons chopped flat leafed Italian parsley
1 tablespoon crumbled mixed Italian seasonings - marjoram and oregano
1/2 cup grated Parmigiano-Reggiano cheese
1/4 cup of milk

Method

1. Set oven at 375F.
2. Warm the oil in a large skillet.
3. Sauté the onion and garlic until soft but not brown.
4. Stir in the tomato sauce and seasonings.
5. If using freshly chopped garden tomatoes, prepare first group of ingredients until sauce thickens.
6. Cut the zucchini into about three long strips each.
7. Lightly sauté the slices in a little oil and garlic.
8. Combine the remaining ingredients until they form a spreadable topping. A bit more milk may be required.
9. Lightly oil a 9˝ by 12˝ baking pan.
10. Spread tomato sauce evenly on the bottom.
11. Lay the strips of zucchini in rows across the width of the dish.
12. Using a spatula, spread the crumb mixture over the zucchini.
13. Bake until surface browns slightly. (about 20 minutes)

Serves 6

Lorraine de Blois

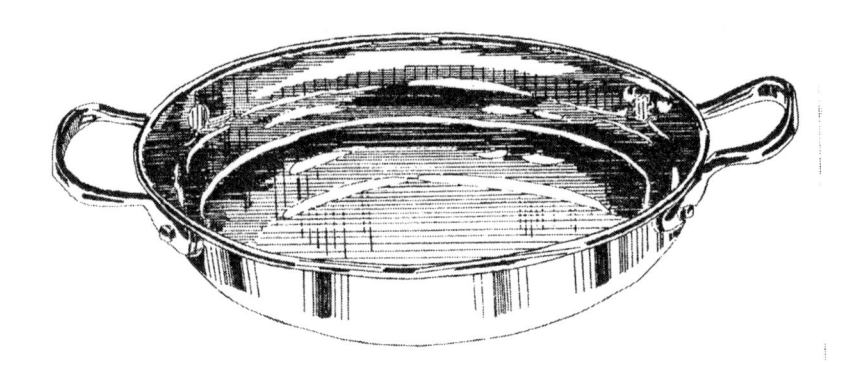

Asparastrata

I have always loved fresh asparagus in the spring but my family sometimes tires of a prolonged menu of steamed spears. In an effort to diversify, I picked up The Asparagus Festival Cookbook (Jan Moore 2003) where I found "Asparastrata Kassandra". A strata is a savoury rendition of a bread pudding. The original recipe is heavier on cheese and eggs than suits our tastes, so I have adapted it into a lower fat version with this result. I don't grow asparagus because the community gardens only allow annuals. I did grow the onions in the community garden and I grew the tarragon in my kitchen.

Ingredients
4 cups of 1 inch cubed whole wheat bread
1 cup of low fat cheddar cheese
1 teaspoon black pepper
1 clove of garlic, crushed
1 finely chopped onion
4 cups of thinly sliced asparagus, cut diagonally
1 cup cottage cheese
4 eggs
2 cups milk
2 teaspoons dried mustard powder
2 teaspoons dried tarragon
1 cup low fat mozzarella cheese

Method
1. Preheat oven to 350F.
2. Mix onion, asparagus, bread, cheddar cheese, pepper and garlic in a bowl.
3. Beat cottage cheese, eggs, milk, tarragon and mustard power in a blender until frothy.
4. Add egg mixture to the dry ingredients in the bowl and mix well.

5. Pour into 9˝ by 13˝ ovenproof pan lightly greased.
6. Top with the mozzarella cheese.
7. Bake in an oven at 350 F for one hour or until golden brown. Let sit for 10 minutes before serving.

Serves 6 hearty appetites for dinner.

JUDITH WARREN

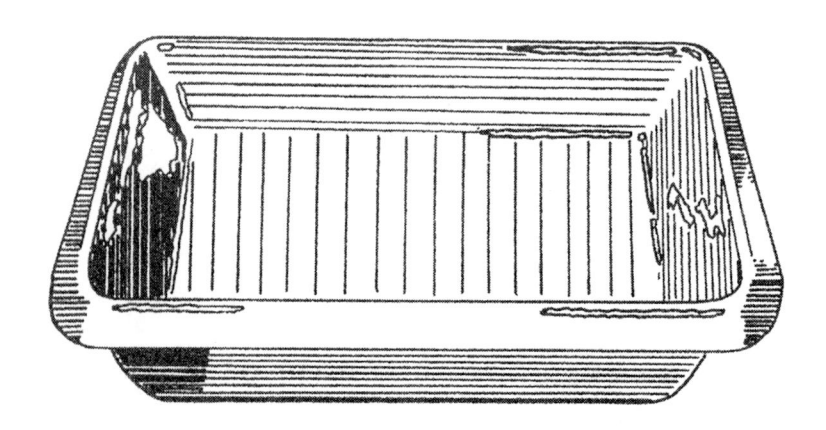

Joey's Potato Pie

The kitchen in my home is typically the domain of my husband Rod, but occasionally I enter. Once a year, I am responsible for hosting a Book Club that is really a terrific excuse for a group of women to get together and drink wine and nosh to our hearts' content. I don't think it's my imagination, but somehow I feel as though there is this unwritten competition when it comes to the food part of our monthly gatherings. I say that because each month, the food just seems to get better and better. If it's really a good night, then we get past the food and on to a hearty book discussion.

This year, I was hosting our Book Club for the novel "The Guernsey Literary and Potato Peel Pie Society" and there wasn't a doubt that I needed to serve a Potato Pie of some sort. Guernsey is in the English Channel that separates France from England and is one of the four Channel Islands close to France. So it is fitting to start with the ingredients for a French onion tart and incorporate potatoes.

Onion and Potato Pie

In nearly every French province, but particularly Alsace-Lorraine, there are recipes for onion tarts, sometimes made with a purée, sometimes with fried onions, green spring onions, or leeks. Some people add bacon, some cream. In Provence the equivalent is the pissaladière, where the already cooked onions are baked on bread dough and garnished with black olives.

Equipment
A 9 inch quiche pan with fluted sides

Ingredients
pastry to line the pan (see recipes and instructions on page 175)
butter for greasing pan
2 tablespoons butter to sweat the onions
1-1/2 lb. of onions

2 eggs
2 oz grated Gruyère cheese
4 or 5 medium potatoes
salt and pepper to taste

Method

1. Set the oven to 375F.
2. Butter the pan and line it with pastry.
3. Partially bake the pastry in the pie dish for several minutes as explained on page 208.
4. Slice the onions fairly fine.
5. Sweat them slowly in the melted butter in a covered pan for about 30 minutes. Keep watch to see that they do not brown. Stir with a wooden fork occasionally. You want them to stay translucent.
6. Peel the potatoes and par-boil them whole for 20 minutes.
7. Beat the eggs in a bowl. Stir in the grated cheese and seasonings.
8. Stir this mixture into the cooked onions.
9. Slice the potatoes.
10. Spread half of the potato slices over the pastry base.
11. Spread the onion/cheese mixture over them.
12. Top the tart with the remaining potato slices in concentric circles.
13. Brush with a little melted butter.
14. Bake for 30 minutes at 375F checking after 25 minutes to make sure it is not browning too quickly.

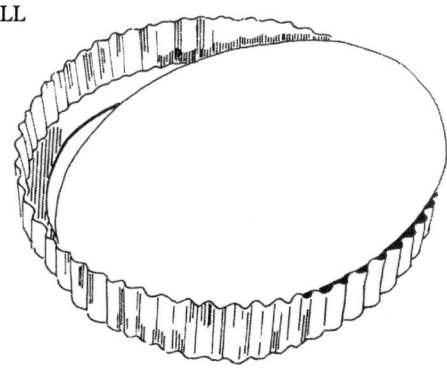

Joey McDowell

Green Tomato Pie

Eighty years ago, in 1929 the conclusion of the famous "persons case" was that the exclusion of women from politics was "a relic of days more barbarous than ours". In 2009 Jane Bigelow was among five London women honoured to mark this anniversary for having made significant contributions to the community over many decades. Having led the way as London's first woman Mayor, Jane has made many contributions to the Woodfield neighbourhood. She lived on Dufferin Avenue for most of her time in elected office and was involved in the organization of the Central London Community Association with another well known Woodfielder, Evelyn Crooks. When she retired it was to a house and garden and a dog on Princess Avenue.

"I can't remember much about cooking when I was mayor," she recalled, "except that I could always make time for baking a pie. This was a family favourite – and still is. The recipe was given to me by an Aunt who had made it for us. I knew after the first bite that I had to have the recipe!"

Ingredients
4 cups of unpeeled green tomatoes cut in 1 inch wedges
1/2 cup sugar
2 tablespoons flour
grated rind of 1 lemon
1/4 teaspoon salt
1 tablespoon fresh lemon juice
3 tablespoons butter
1/4 teaspoon allspice
pastry for a 9 inch pie shell and a lattice top (see page 175)

Method

Preheat oven to 350 F.

1. Mix flour, sugar, lemon rind, spice and salt together.
2. Sprinkle a little on the bottom of a 9 inch unbaked pie shell.
3. Arrange tomato wedges in the pie shell a layer at a time and cover each layer with a little lemon juice and dot with butter.
4. Sprinkle each layer with the sugar and flour mixture.
5. When layers are complete cover with pastry lattice shell.
6. Bake for 45 minutes.

Jane Bigelow

Spinach Pie (Spanakopita)

Our family lived in Crete, Greece in 1997 while my husband worked at the university's research facility. Our children were 2, 4 and 6 at the time. We ate delicious spanakopita from corner stands in the big city of Iraklion. In Agia Pelagia, we lived surrounded by fields of greens and used them to make this recipe for spanakopita.

We moved to London, Ontario on Canada Day, 1998. We often make spanakopita to remind us of our time in Greece. It is a favourite when we have friends over for a Greek meal.

While we brought back many cookbooks from Crete, our favourite is from the Athens publisher Efstathiadis called "The Best Book of Greek Cookery" by Chrissa Paradissis. It has 5 different recipes for spinach pies. The recipe below is adapted from that book, which is now held together with an elastic band, as the pages have all come loose.

Since we grow spinach and swiss chard in our Woodfield backyard, we often use a combination of these in this pie. It works well with just swiss chard too.

We usually buy our feta from our Arabic corner store, just up the street on Adelaide and Elias. They have a selection of feta cheeses and we enjoy trying different kinds. They also sell the best Kalamata olives, so we are regulars there.

Equipment
You'll need a 10" by 14" by 2" baking dish. A pastry brush is also needed.

Ingredients
2 lb. fresh spinach (or fresh swiss chard, or mixture) washed and torn/chopped
1 lb. feta cheese, crumbled
2 eggs, beaten

1 to 2 green onions, chopped finely
1 teaspoon dried oregano or 3 teaspoons fresh oregano, chopped finely
1 teaspoon freshly ground pepper
1 package of frozen phyllo pastry, thawed still in package
1 cup Cretan or other Greek olive oil

Method

1. Wash spinach well, drain and tear/chop into small pieces. Squeeze excess water from spinach and place in large mixing bowl.
2. Add chopped green onions (or chives), chopped oregano, ground pepper, and crumbled feta cheese.
3. Beat the 2 eggs well, and add to mixture. Toss gently. Set aside.

Assembly

Do not open the thawed phyllo pastry until you are ready to assemble or it will dry out.

As you work, have a clean dish towel on hand to cover pastry sheets to keep them from drying out. Make sure your work area is dry, too much moisture causes the sheets to stick together.

1. Preheat oven to 375F.
2. Place 1 cup of olive oil in a bowl, have your pastry brush at hand, as well as the finished spinach filling.
3. Brush the baking dish with olive oil. Add 8 to 10 phyllo sheets, one at a time, brushing each layer with olive oil. You can place a folded sheet into the dish, if it fits more easily that way.
4. Spread the spinach filling evenly. Cover with remaining phyllo sheets, being sure to brush each layer with olive oil, including the top layer.
5. Score completed pie into 2 to 3 inch pieces, use a sharp knife and cut down several layers to ease serving later.
6. Before placing in oven, sprinkle top layer lightly with water to prevent drying out. Bake uncovered, 40 to 45 minutes. Cool slightly to let set, cut in squares. Serve hot or cold.

Makes 16 to 20 pieces.

Everyone in our family has helped make spanakopita. When my husband Brian makes the pie, he patiently layers the phyllo pastry and filling so that there are two layers of spinach. I tend to move quickly through the kitchen, and so put the filling in all at once!

Our children have always loved to make spanakopitakia - the little spinach pies, often in a triangle shape, perfect for appetizers. We use the same frozen phyllo sheets, but cut them in long rectangular ribbons. A spoonful of spinach filling is placed at the bottom corner of 2 ribbons of pastry, and then folded over to meet the opposite corner, which makes a triangle shape at the bottom of your long ribbon. The triangle gets folded left, and right, so that the filling is rolled up. Brush with olive oil and bake on a cookie sheet for 10 to 15 minutes until golden brown. The frozen phyllo packages often have illustrations to make triangle appetizers inside.

LINDA BUSSIÈRE

Baked Beans

Peggy Curnoe is the fourth generation of her family to live in the Woodfield area. Her great-grandfather, George Braund, bought land on Palace Street in 1854, just a few years after it was surveyed. Glen and Peggy's children grew up in the Ontario cottage on Cartwright Street and son Aaron currently lives in an apartment here, making him a fifth generation Woodfielder.

Peggy is currently a case manager for The Community Care Access Centre.

Equipment

A Dutch oven for soaking and boiling the beans then an earthenware bean pot for simmering them would be ideal. But you can do everything in a large enamelled cast iron pot.

Ingredients

1 pound white navy or pea beans. Hensall, the White Bean Capital of Canada, is close enough to us that you can use this superior local bean.
1 medium onion sliced
1/2 tablespoon salt
2 teaspoons cider vinegar
1/2 teaspoon prepared mustard or 1/4 teaspoon powdered mustard
1 tablespoon brown sugar
1/4 cup mild-flavoured molasses
1 14 ounce jar of tomato sauce or a 24 ounce can of stewed tomatoes
a pinch of black pepper
2 or 3 cloves of garlic, peeled and chopped
3 whole cloves (spice)

METHOD
1. Soak beans, covered in water overnight.
2. Drain. Add fresh water to cover.
3. Add garlic.
4. Bring to a boil.
5. Skim off any surface scum.
6. Simmer until tender.
7. Drain, reserving liquid if needed towards the end of baking.
8. Add all remaining ingredients.
9. Bake at 325F for three hours.

Peggy remembers: *This is a recipe that my room mate and I used to make when we didn't have much money. We often served it to friends.*

PEGGY CURNOE

Lentils alla Turca

This is a dish that I got from a fellow graduate student from Turkey. It makes a nice change from curried lentils.

Ingredients

1 cup lentils
5 cups water
1 large onion
2 small carrots
1 large potato
juice of a medium sized lemon
garlic to taste (about 4 cloves)
1 tablespoon tomato paste
2 teaspoons salt
4 tablespoons olive oil or less
1 tablespoon dried mint

Method

1. Soak lentils in 3 cups water overnight (or boil for 5 minutes in the morning)
2. Cook for 30 to 40 minutes until tender.
3. Add garlic, chopped onion, diced carrots, potato, tomato paste, oil, salt and 1 to 2 cups water* and cook for another 20 minutes or until vegetables are tender.
4. Cool, add mint and lemon juice**
5. Serve at room temperature.

* maybe less, depending on the lentils. You want to end up with a stew, not soup.
** start with half the amount and taste it to see if you need more.

Very good with pita chips

Regina Moorcroft

Tom's Jalapenos Rellenos

Most of us know Tom Benner as an artist of national stature and the guy who put a rhino on the lawn of the Art Gallery. Few locals are aware of his stint as the cook in a Mexican restaurant. Not just any old restaurant, but behind the counter of the Clarenden, London's original Town Hall, later known as the Blue Boot, at the corner of Talbot and King Streets. It was a funky diner type of spot, with a hatch into the bar through which Tom slid plates of the best quesadillas and nachos in town. Tom has travelled to Mexico six or seven times. He loves the people and the food and the colours of the country, which he captures in his paintings.

One summer he stayed on Pelee Island, serving up Mexican food from a beach hut, while constructing a sculpture of seven dolphins, which now sweep in an arc out over the waterfront of Sault Ste. Marie.

Expect this recipe to deliver authentic flavours along with a kick.

Equipment
Keep a supply of the latex surgical gloves (available in drug stores) to pull on before handling peppers. Do not touch your face at any time with the juice of cut peppers on the gloves or your hands. You will need a blender.

Ingredients for the sauce
2 tablespoons of butter
1 large onion
3 large garlic cloves
2 cans diced tomatoes
2 or 3 (depending on how much heat you like) chopped jalapeno peppers
3 canned chipotle peppers
1 lime
Frank's Hot Sauce

2 or 3 handfuls of corn tortilla chips

Ingredients for filling

24 good-sized jalapeno peppers
4 to 5 cups of medium cheddar cheese and Monterey Jack combined
sour cream
green onions
flat tortillas

Method (start the day before you intend to serve)

1. Blacken the 24 jalapeno peppers, using a wire rack on a gas stove top, or on a bbq.
2. Immerse in cold water for a minute.
3. Pull on rubber gloves. Skin, quarter and hull the peppers.
4. Place in cold salt water overnight.
5. Meanwhile, prepare the Red Sauce:
6. Chop the onion and garlic and sauté in the butter until just translucent.
7. Add the diced tomatoes, the 2 or 3 chopped (need gloves again) fresh jalapenos with skins on, and the 3 canned chipotle peppers. The more seeds you include, the hotter it gets.
8. Squeeze in juice from 1 lime.
9. Shake in some Frank's Hot Sauce (to taste).
10. Bring to a boil and simmer for a few minutes.
11. Crush the corn tortilla chips with a rolling pin or in a food processor. Add to the sauce.
12. Cool the mixture then process it in a blender. Be careful it doesn't blow the lid off!
13. Return to saucepan and simmer for one hour.

Assembly

14. Preheat the oven to 350F.
15. Grate the cheese.
16. Place the red sauce in the bottom of several small oven proof bowls.
17. Layer 4 or 5 of the skinned jalapenos on top of the sauce.
18. Add more red sauce then cover with cheese.
19. Place in a 350F oven until the cheese bubbles.

To Serve

Char 8 to 10 tortilla shells. Fill each with a scoop of the mixture. Garnish with a spoon of extra red sauce (if you want), a dollop of sour cream, and chopped green onions.

Roll and enjoy.

Tom Benner

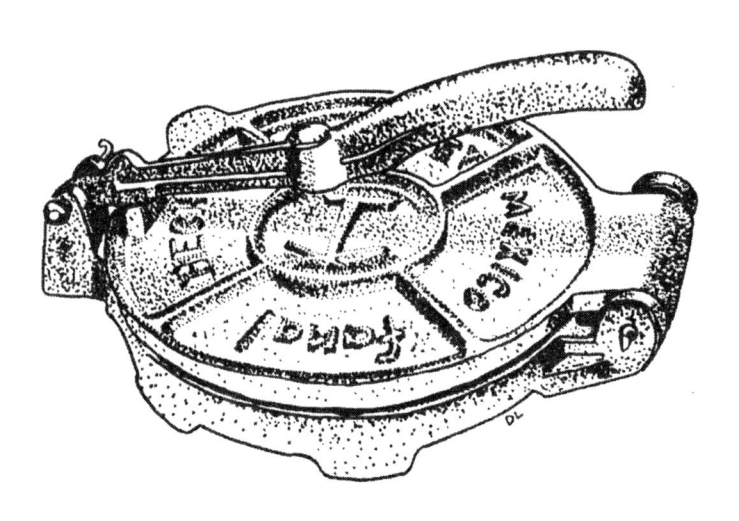

PASTA

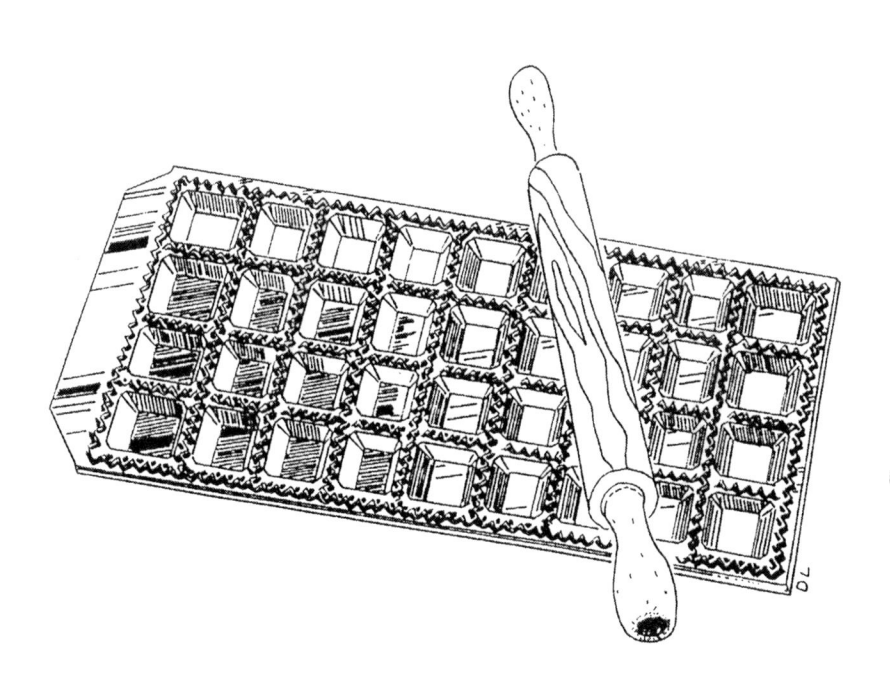

Pasta with Lobster and Chilies

My sister Emma and I have many memories of time spent with our dad, Chris Squire, in his restaurant, the Auberge du Petit Prince. One of our funniest experiences, and of course the one that parents have to tell, involves live lobsters let loose to chase us around the kitchen. We still call them "Lobbers" and we still find them scary. Little did we know they would make such a tasty sauce!

Ingredients

2 – 2 lb. lobsters
4 tablespoons sea salt
8 bay leaves
8 cloves garlic, halved
4 small chilies, cut in half
1/4 teaspoon dried red pepper flakes
juice of 1 lemon
1/2 teaspoon minced garlic
1/2 cup extra virgin olive oil
1 lb. fettuccini or other thin pasta
1/2 cup minced parsley
2 cups of cooked spring vegetables for garnish (asparagus, sugar peas, sweet peppers)

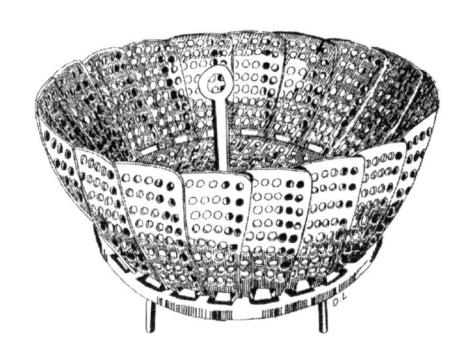

Method

1. Fill a large pot with water (a minimum of 6 quarts) and add the bay leaves, garlic cloves, 2 tablespoons of the salt and the chilies and bring to a boil.
2. Take the live lobsters and cut along the centre line of the head section with a sharp knife.
3. Drop the lobsters into the boiling water and cook for 6 minutes.
4. Remove the lobsters from the boiling water, chill quickly in ice water and when cool, remove the meat from the tail, claws and knuckles.
5. Bring another pot of water to the boil for the pasta and add 2 tablespoons of salt.
6. In a serving bowl, combine the red pepper flakes, lemon juice, the minced garlic and the olive oil .
7. Cut the lobster meat into large bite-sized chunks. Add the lobster to the bowl and let it sit while you cook the pasta.
8. At this point, add your spring vegetables.
9. When you are ready to serve, cook the pasta until it just reaches al dente.
10. Drain quickly and toss with the lobster, oil, lemon, garlic, spring vegetables and pepper flakes. Season with ground pepper as required.
11. To garnish, sprinkle with freshly cut Italian parsley and a drizzle of your best olive oil.

Under no cicumstances should you add cheese as it overwhelms the delicate flavour of the lobster.

Serves 4

Josie Squire

From Ann McColl's Kitchen Shop

If you are making pasta for the first time, you might find it easier to make a smaller amount. This recipe was given out with our hand-cranked pasta machines at Ann McColl's Kitchen Shop.

No dried pasta from a cellophane package can come close to the nourishing, velvety smoothness of properly made egg pasta. It is a mother's embrace. And as easy to give.

All you need is a flat surface, the counter top is fine, a fork and a cut-down broom handle, or long, narrow pasta rolling pin. In the centre of the space, pile one and one half cups fine Semolina flour or hard wheat (Durham) all-purpose flour. It is easier to start with this small amount until you get the mixing technique down. Add a pinch of salt. Twirl your finger around in the centre to make a crater like the top of Vesuvius. Drop in two medium size eggs, 1 teaspoon olive oil, and 1 teaspoon warm water, at room temperature. Use the fork to swish them with the surrounding flour, supporting the sides with your other hand, until you gradually amalgamate all of it into the eggs and you have a sticky ball of dough. If it refuses to hold together, dab on a very few drops of water. Sprinkle the board lightly with flour and begin a vigorous ten minutes of kneading, until the ball of dough is smooth. Cover it with a bowl so that you and the pasta can both take a ten minute break before the rolling begins.

Apply pressure along the elongated wooden pin, rolling in all directions until a thickness of one eighth inch is achieved. Keep going until it is almost as thin as a dime. Let it have another rest for fifteen minutes. Give it a gentle rub with flour before folding the sheet over and over into a four inch wide long flat roll. Cut into one quarter inch strips, shake them loose, and you have fettuccini. The flat dough could be fashioned into ravioli by using a partitioned tray or a crimped press or cut in wide strips for lasagna.

This time-honoured process can be updated by whirling the flour and eggs in a food processor then passing the resulting ball through the rollers of a steel tabletop hand pasta machine. When it is thin enough, proceed to one of the two cutting blades. A customer once brought me in a photograph of her three-year old son turning the handle to make noodles. Once you have mastered pasta making, you can ruin it by overcooking. Fill a pot, larger than four quarts, with water. Once it comes to the boil, add salt then drop in your fresh noodles a handful at a time. Watch the pot come back to the boil, give it four or five minutes until you see your pasta float to the top. Use a long wooden fork to gently stir and to lift up strands to check if it is done to the point where you can bite through with a little resistance. Avoid mushy. Commercial pasta takes twice as long to cook.

ANN MCCOLL LINDSAY

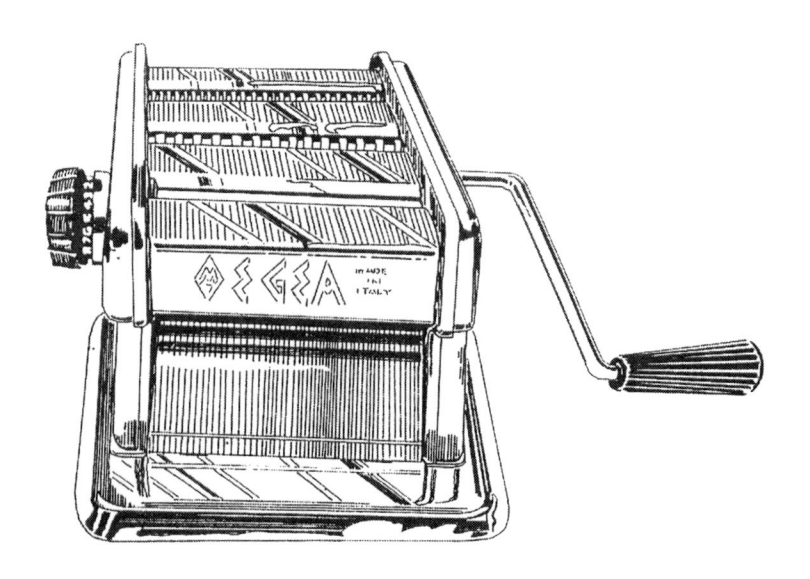

Spinach (or Swiss Chard) Lasagna

Some of us who have sown rather too many rows of it in the Carling Heights community garden, use Swiss chard instead of spinach. It is equally delicious. "Soften" the chard leaves, torn up with whatever water clings to them after washing, in batches in the microwave or steamer. This dish was among several served by Christine Troughton at a Mama Mia lasagna-tasting porch party held in Woodfield.

Ingredients
1 large onion, peeled and chopped
2 tablespoons olive oil
2 garlic cloves, crushed
2 lbs. cooked, fresh spinach or chard, chopped
2 lbs. ricotta cheese
salt and freshly ground black pepper
1 large jar Italian tomato sauce
1/2 lb mozzarella cheese
9 sheets of lasagna
butter for greasing

Method
1. Preheat oven to 400 F.
2. Grease a large, shallow ovenproof dish.
3. Sauté the onion in the olive oil in a large saucepan for 10 minutes, until soft not browned.
4. Add garlic and cook for a minute. Remove from heat.
5. Squeeze excess liquid out of the cooked or thawed spinach, then add to the onion mixture, together with the ricotta cheese, salt and lots of freshly ground black pepper.
6. Cover the dish with a thin layer of tomato sauce.
7. Put a layer of lasagne on top, followed by a layer of the spinach mixture.

8. Thinly slice 1/2 cup of the mozzarella. Make a layer of mozzarella slices, then of tomato sauce.
9. Continue like this until all the ingredients are used up, ending with a layer of sauce.
10. Grate the remaining cheese and arrange in 3 lines on the top.
11. Bake for 1 hour, covering the dish with foil after 40 or 45 minutes if the top begins to get too brown.

Serves 8

CHRISTINE TROUGHTON

SPAGHETTINI CON PISELLI

Rod McDowell really enjoys experimenting in his kitchen. He ran across the street, very excited about this new light, thin pasta sauce he had discovered. Its strength lies in its versatility.

INGREDIENTS
8 ounces of angel hair, capellini #1, or thin spaghettini
3 cloves of garlic
1/2 of a sweet onion
4 strips of bacon
1-1/2 cups of stock (vegetable or seafood - see supplier list)
1-1/2 cups freshly shucked or frozen peas
1 tablespoon olive oil and 2 teaspoons butter
pepper and parsley
Parmigiano-Reggiano for grating on top

METHOD
1. Put large pot of water on to boil for the pasta.
2. Shuck or defrost the peas.
3. Cook bacon crisp. Cool then chop.
4. Dice the onion, crush or mince the garlic and sauté a few minutes in the fat rendered from the bacon slices.
5. Pour in the stock and boil to reduce.
6. Add the peas to the stock and simmer for a couple of minutes.
7. Boil the pasta for 4 minutes as thin pasta cooks quickly.
8. Drain pasta and return to pot.
9. Toss pasta in butter and oil.
10. Add stock/pea mixture and toss gently.
11. Divide onto warmed serving plates. Top with crumbled bacon, grated cheese and parsley.

ROD MCDOWELL

MAKE THIS RECIPE YOUR OWN

This dish really lends itself to seafood. Try laying a circle of grilled or boiled shrimp on top of the pasta, or fresh scallops. Italians do not pass the cheese when seafood is a part of the pasta course. A lobster bouillon, available at our Covent Garden Market, is a good substitute for the stock if you are introducing the seafood.

Bolognese Sauce

A couple of times a year I like to treat myself to hearty and traditional Italian pasta sauce filled with meats. Many of us are conscious of eating a healthy Mediterranean diet which tends to exclude meats in favour of fish, but I'm confident this recipe from the Northern part of Italy will satisfy you.

Equipment
food processor
sauté pan

Ingredients
1 tablespoon olive oil
1 tablespoon butter
2 medium onions, finely chopped
1 stalk celery, finely diced
2 carrots, diced
4 cloves garlic, minced
1/2 lb ground veal
1/2 lb hot pork sausages (see supplier list)
one small can of tomato paste
1 cup any white wine
1 – 28 oz can Italian plum tomatoes preferably San Marzano
1 cup milk
Freshly grated Parmigiano-Reggiano cheese

Method
1. Chop the vegetables and garlic in the processor.
2. Heat the olive oil, add the butter then sauté the vegetables and garlic about 4 to 5 minutes stirring constantly.
3. Remove the meat from the sausage casings, add along with the ground veal to the vegetables.

4. Continue cooking everything together until meats are no longer pink, break the meats with a wooden spoon as you stir.
5. Add the tomato paste, wine and tomatoes. I pulse the tomatoes two or three times in the food processor before adding. Stir in a couple of pinches of salt.
6. Reduce heat, cover and simmer about an hour or longer stir occasionally.
7. About 20 minutes before serving, add the milk and check to see if it needs any salt or pepper. The hot pork sausages give it a good kick so pepper usually isn't required.

I prefer this sauce spooned over a bowl of spaghetti and sprinkled with grated Parmigiano-Reggiano cheese.

Serves 8

ROD MCDOWELL

Sarah's Spaghetti Sauce

In **At the Corner of Hope** (*a novel set in Woodfield*), *Sarah is a student at UWO. Her one-and-only specialty is spaghetti with tomato sauce. Early in the book Sarah offers to produce a spaghetti supper for her visiting aunts and for Matt, who is turning an old Woodfield house into a Bed & Breakfast operation. At that point, alas, the would-be B&B has no stove. So Matt, our hero, goes along Colborne Street to "Deke's Variety" (aka Pete's), buys two big cans of Spaghetti-O's and heats supper in the microwave. Not a good substitute for the rich homemade sauce that Sarah cooks up near the end of the book!* "Spaghetti — still her specialty — with a rich sauce made of plum tomatoes simmered with onions, peppers, spices, and lots of garlic. The kitchen swirled with wonderful odours. . . ."

A fictional feast – but a happy one! Pasta is always a comfort food for busy people. In the 1950s, when we lived with our five children at the corner of Dufferin and William, there were no pizza parlours – but we could always count on spaghetti for a quick and happy supper. Now that we have vegetarians in our family, Sarah's recipe has the added value of being meatless. Artichoke hearts are the secret ingredient in Sarah's sauce.

Equipment
You need a big saucepan for the sauce, for fear it boils over. If you use fresh tomatoes, you will need the pan full of boiling water to scald them in, and a bowl of ice water to drop them into, so the skins come off easily.

Ingredients
1/4 cup of olive oil
2 medium onions, chopped
2 cloves of garlic, minced

1 sweet red pepper, chopped
1/2 teaspoon dried basil
1/2 teaspoon dried oregano
1 tablespoon crushed black peppercorns
1/2 teaspoon salt
1 pinch of cayenne (or red pepper flakes)
2 lb. of plum tomatoes: or 28 oz. can of plum tomatoes
2 6oz. jars of artichoke hearts, marinated in oil.
2 lb. of spaghetti

Method

1. If tomatoes are in season, fill the saucepan with boiling water. Drop in the fresh plum tomatoes, a few at a time for 10 seconds to scald them, then transfer to a bowl of cold water and slip off their skins. Using a big can of plum tomatoes is an easier option.
2. Heat olive oil in the large saucepan. Add the oil marinade drained from the artichoke hearts. Sauté onions and chopped red pepper over medium-low heat for 10 minutes. Add garlic, spices, salt and pepper and sauté for 1 minute.
3. Add the tomatoes. Simmer for 30 minutes. (Less, if using the canned plum tomatoes: about 15 minutes.)
4. Add the drained artichoke hearts. Simmer for another 10 minutes (while the spaghetti cooks in a separate pot).

Serve with grated parmesan cheese, a bottle of Chianti, and fresh bread from the Portuguese baker on Adelaide street.

Serves 6

Elizabeth Waterston,
Colborne Street (near the corner of Hope).

Note: Elizabeth is the author of **At the Corner of Hope**, *the book referred to in the recipe.*

Pasta with Tuna and Black Olives

When John Thorp and his wife Bonnie took a sabbatical year in Rome, they had an apartment near the ancient Forum, with good access to the colourful Roman markets. They ate as the Romans do, creatively, using age-old combinations of ingredients. This pasta dish is not for the faint of heart. It is a blend of robust Mediterranean flavours. Do not be afraid of the anchovies. They heighten the seafood taste of the tuna.

Ingredients
- 2 - 3.5 ounce tins of solid chunk tuna
- 12 Kalamata olives, pitted and sliced
- 4 to 6 cloves of garlic
- 6 anchovy fillets
- 1/2 cup of fruity olive oil
- 1/2 cup of flat Italian parsley
- salt and pepper to taste
- Pasta for four to six people - fettuccine, rotini, spaghetti, capellini - your choice

Method
1. In a small bowl, break up the tuna with a fork.
2. Cut the anchovies into 1/4 inch pieces.
3. Blend the olive slices, minced garlic and anchovies into the tuna.
4. Stir in enough olive oil to make a fairly thick sauce.
5. Mince the parsley and turn it into the sauce.
6. Cover the bowl and let it stand to infuse the flavours for an hour or two at room temperature.
7. Boil the pasta according to package directions or under 5 minutes if fresh.
8. Drain. Return to pot. Incorporate sauce ingredients.

When served with the thin angel hair pasta, this dish evokes memories of linguini with clams, garlic and parsley, eaten in a coastal Mediterranean town.

JOHN THORP

Co-operative Pasta

Although Woodfielders appreciate local produce, they do not have a grocery store in their community. But we do have a very special co-operative food store just on our Adelaide Street boundary at Princess Avenue. The London Co-op Store began in 1970 when a group of people got together in order to buy food and dry goods in bulk that was good for them and the planet.

Founding members included artists Greg Curnoe and Bob Bozak. Originally the Co-op members ordered their food, had it delivered to their front porch and got together to sort and package what each household had ordered. They came to the current store over twenty years ago and now provide the members with food that is as free as possible from additives, preservatives, pesticides and herbicides. This year the Co-op celebrates forty years of solid community service.

Barbara Jones Warwick is a member of the Board and Provisions Committee.

She is sharing her recipe for an original pasta dish made with Co-op produce.

Presto Pasta Verdi

This is a fairly quick dish that is full of vitamins, minerals, fibre and (if made with whole grain pasta) complex carbohydrates.

Ingredients
- 4 cups chopped onion
- 2 tablespoons olive or avocado oil
- 1/2 tsp salt
- 8 cups chopped greens (my favourites are a combination of Swiss chard, including the stems, and dinosaur kale, stems removed;

spinach may be substituted for the chard or collards for the kale)
3/4 lb extruded pasta such as penne or spirals that will "catch" the sauce
3/4 lb feta cheese, crumbled or grated
1/4 cup pesto (either jarred or home made - recipe follows)
freshly ground pepper to taste

Method

1. Put the pasta water on to boil. Chop onions, wash and chop the greens.
   TIP keep packages of chopped, blanched kale on hand in the freezer and add them to this or any other dish requiring kale.
2. Heat oil in a large, heavy bottomed pan over medium heat. Add the onions, the greens, and sprinkle with salt. Stir so that oil and salt are evenly distributed and reduce heat to low. Cover and let veggies wilt or melt. This should take about ten minutes, about the same time as it takes to cook the pasta.
   TIP This wilting method allows you to get the effect of sautéing with less fat.
3. Add the pasta when the water has come to a boil. Cook to al dente stage. Drain.
4. Toss together the cooked veggies, pasta, feta and pesto. Season with pepper to taste.

OPTIONS: Chopped green or yellow zucchini can replace some of the greens. Sweet red pepper (up to a cup) can be added for a little colour. Chopped bulb fennel can replace some of the onion for additional flavour (up to a cup). Add any of these optional items at the same time you would cook the other veggies.

Serves 6

Pesto

This recipe omits the cheese so that you may add it at cooking and serving time. If you are choosing to freeze the pesto, it means you take up less freezer space and have fresh cheese at serving time. In addition to the traditional Reggiano, or Parmesan, try Romano for a stronger taste and Asiago for a milder, nuttier taste.

Ingredients
- 1 oz (1/8 cup) toasted pine nuts (sunflower seeds may be substituted where nut allergies are a concern)
- 1 cup tightly packed, cleaned basil leaves
- 1 to 2 cloves garlic, minced (depending on size and your relationship with garlic)
- 1/4 cup olive oil (fruity olive oil imparts a lovely flavour)
- 1/4 teaspoon salt (optional)

Method
1. Toast pine nuts at 300F for 5 to 10 minutes until they start to get golden and their aroma seeps out into the kitchen.
2. Place all ingredients in a food processor and process until a smooth paste is formed.
3. Either use immediately, refrigerate for up to three days or freeze in an ice cube tray and pop pesto cubes into a zip lock bag so you can use them whenever you need a little pesto.

Barbara Jones Warwick

Hot Penne Pasta

This is a pasta recipe Jeff and I have made since we were married. It is a favourite with house guests and friends. Some call it "Kate's Pasta." It is also very good cold.

Ingredients

1 tablespoon red wine vinegar
6 tablespoons olive oil
1/4 teaspoon dried red pepper flakes
1/8 teaspoon coarsely ground black pepper
1 minced clove of garlic
1 16 oz tin of plum tomatoes, reserve some of the juice. If using fresh tomatoes, blanch and peel
1/4 to 1/2 lb mozzarella cheese
3 oz sliced black forest ham or prosciutto
1/4 cup of lightly packed fresh basil; dried basil or marjoram could also be used but cut the amount in half. Dried has a more mellow flavour, which I prefer in the winter.
12 oz penne or rotini, the spiral pasta which captures the great sauce

Method

1. In a bowl, whisk together vinegar, pepper, and garlic. If using dried herbs, stir into the oil mixture. If using fresh basil, thinly slice then set aside.
2. Coarsely chop plum tomatoes, set aside.
3. Cube cheese (1/2 inch) and chop ham. Set aside.
4. Cook pasta and drain. Do not rinse.
5. Toss in oil mixture, then cheese, ham and tomatoes. Stir well. Add some of the tomato juice if a sauce texture is preferred. If the cheese is not melting, put back on the burner on low for a few minutes, stir.
6. When done, toss in fresh basil.

7. Serve. Goes well with a dry Rhine or a light red wine.

KATE RAPSON AND JEFF CARSON

Cold Tomato Sauce and Hot Pasta

This recipe has travelled around Woodfield. It originated with Rosie Donovan, who with husband Alistair, organized annual Morris Dancing parties right down the centre of Prospect Avenue. Beer and food followed on their porch. When the Browns retired to Britain, the recipe was passed along to Joan Smith who gave it to Christine Troughton who is sharing it with us all.

Equipment
A blender or processor is needed for a smooth sauce. You could also just stir all ingredients in a large bowl for a chunkier version.

Ingredients
3 cups diced tomatoes
2 cups sweet onions
1 to 2 teaspoons minced garlic
1/3 cup chopped basil
3 tablespoons chopped parsley
1/8 cup balsamic vinegar
salt and freshly ground pepper
1/4 cup olive oil
spaghetti or noodles
freshly grated parmesan cheese
cubed or grated mozzarella

Method
1. Lightly fry onion and garlic in a little oil.
2. Combine all of the sauce ingredients in a food processor or blender or mix in a large bowl.
3. Cook pasta then drain into a large serving bowl.
4. Toss mozzarella into it so that it melts.
5. Pour the tomato sauce over the pasta.
6. Top with parmesan.

CHRISTINE TROUGHTON

SEAFOOD

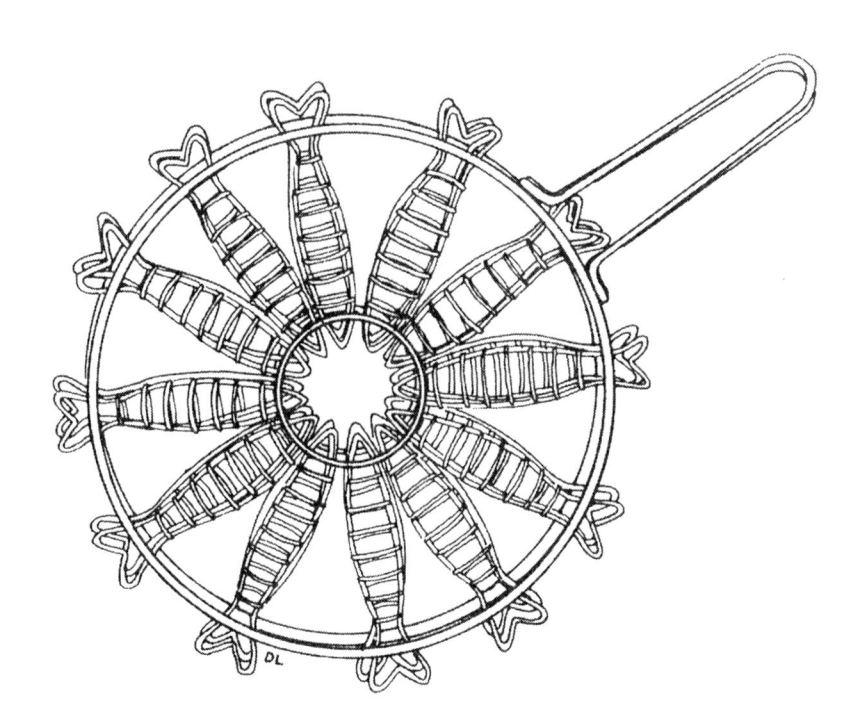

Steamed Fish

Shadylawn, Judy Elliot's house on Palace Street, has become home for countless overseas students over the years. Many consider her a surrogate parent. Haiyun Chen enjoys cooking in spite of the limitations of student digs. Judy welcomes him into the Shadylawn kitchen where they try out his Chinese favourites.

Equipment
Improvise a steamer by placing a roasting rack into a large frying pan or wok. You will need a large lid to cover this pan and a long stainless platter or shallow ovenproof dish in which to place the fish.

Ingredients
4 fillets of frozen sole, cod, or haddock. Haiyun prefers fresh, whole fish, such as red snapper or grouper, when he can find it. (see supplier list at the back of the book)
3 inch piece of fresh ginger root
3 scallions
1/4 to 1/2 cup of light soy sauce, according to your taste
1/2 cup of peanut oil

Method
1. Peel the ginger root and cut it into thin matchstick pieces.
2. Julienne the scallions into the same thin three inch long pieces.
3. Place half of the ginger strips in the baking dish. Set the fish on top. Spread the other half over the fish.
4. Set the rack in your fry pan with water under it. Place pan with fish on top of rack. Cover. Bring to a boil then adjust to a medium simmer. Steam for 10 to 15 minutes depending on the thickness of the fish. Test with a fork at the widest section. It should flake easily and have lost its gelatinous appearance.
5. While the fish is steaming, prepare the sauce. Warm the Tamari

soy gently. Heat the oil in a small frypan until it is quite hot. Drop the scallion slivers into the oil for a minute. Mix the warm soy with the hot oil.
6. Remove fish with a slotted spatula to a platter. Pour sauce over and eat as soon as possible.

SERVING SUGGESTIONS:

Place fish on a bed of rice before dressing with sauce. Serve with blanched, whole baby bok choy.

HAIYUN CHEN

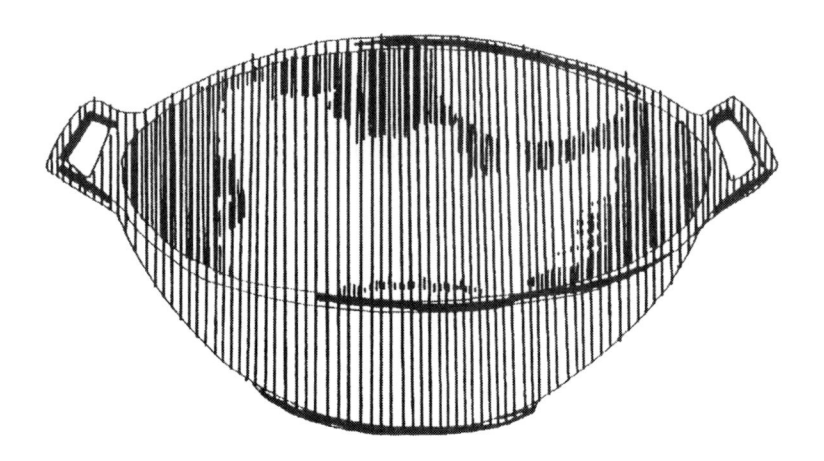

Salmon with Secret Dill Sauce

I once went to a restaurant in Ottawa and ate a fantastic salmon dish. The secret was in the sauce that was draped over it. I was haunted by that dish and tried to duplicate it and came up with this succulent recipe. This dish can be made on the barbecue or in the oven.

Ingredients
1-1/2 lb salmon fillet
juice of 1 lemon
coarse sea salt & fresh ground pepper to taste
olive oil

For sauce
1/4 cup mayonnaise (I use Hellman's light)
1/4 cup plain yogurt 2% fat and up (do not use no fat).
1 level teaspoon Dijon mustard
1 heaped tablespoon dry dill weed or preferably 2 tablespoons of fresh dill.
1/2 teaspoon olive oil

Method
1. Preheat oven to 400F.
2. For barbecue, place salmon on double thickness greased foil with skin side down
3. For oven, place salmon on greased oven proof dish with skin side down
4. Squirt lemon juice on salmon.
5. Sprinkle with salt and pepper.
6. Drizzle olive oil over fish.
7. Cook at 400F in oven uncovered. Cook until salmon is almost cooked - about 15 minutes. Do not turn salmon over.
8. Mix sauce ingredients together and drape on salmon .

9. In oven, broil until sauce is slightly crisp and golden.
10. If cooking on barbecue cook a little longer until sauce is as above.
11. Lift the fillet off the skin before serving.

Serves 2 to 3

Francine Lacroix
Owner/Manager
Queen's Village for Seniors

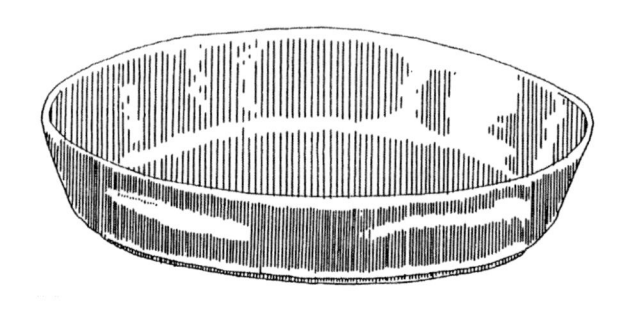

Annie's Sole

My grandmother, Annie McColl, poached sole in milk on a large black coal stove in war-time Glasgow. It was a delicate dish, prepared for those feeling poorly. Dover sole is the most flavourful, but lemon sole is less expensive. We considered lemon sole a special treat.

Ingredients
a sole fillet for each person
butter for the pan and a knob for the sauce
a cup or more of milk or light cream
salt, white pepper, parsley
a lemon

Method
1. Preheat the oven to 350F.
2. Butter an oval or rectangular baker.
3. Lay slices of sole on the dish.
4. Sprinkle with salt and white pepper.
5. Dot with butter.
6. Pour on sufficient milk or light cream to almost cover the fillets.
7. Bake for just under 10 minutes, depending on amount and thickness of fish.
8. Sprinkle chopped fresh parsley on top, and lemon wedges.
9. Serve with small, boiled potatoes tossed in butter.

Annie McColl

Comfy Fish Pie

Helen and Benedict Lockwood took up residence in Woodfield after living 22 years in Arlesheim, Switzerland. They enjoyed preparing meals for new friends there, and when it came time to leave, several requested copies of his favourite recipes. So Benedict printed a small collection in December of 2008 which he is now sharing with his new neighbours. This fish pie is Helen's favourite comfort food on cold evenings. After trying this dish, it is becoming one of ours too.

Equipment
a 9˝ or 10˝ oval au gratin oven baker

Ingredients
1 lb. of a firm white fish, such as haddock or cod. In Switzerland, Benedict used frozen Dorsch fillets.
1/4 lb. small precooked shrimp
1 cup of milk
1 medium onion
1/2 cup of grated Gruyere cheese
3 or 4 medium potatoes
1-1/2 tablespoons butter for the roux
2 tablespoons of butter for the mashed potatoes
plus extra for buttering the dish
1-1/2 tablespoons of flour
nutmeg, salt and pepper

Method
1. Preheat oven to 350F.
2. Defrost the fish if frozen.
3. Butter the shallow baking dish.
4. Peel the potatoes and put them on to boil.
5. Poach the fish in the milk with the onion cut into quarters and a

sprinkling of salt and pepper. It should take about 10 minutes on a gentle heat.
6. Lift the fillets out with a perforated spatula or large serving spoon. Place them in a single layer in the baker. Add the shrimp on top.
7. Sprinkle with a little nutmeg and the grated cheese.
8. Strain the milk into a bowl. Add the onions to the fish.
9. Make a roux (white sauce) by melting the butter in a small heavy saucepan. Stir in the flour to make a paste. Whisk in the warmed milk and continue stirring until a smooth sauce consistency is achieved.
10. Pour this sauce over the fish.
11. Mash the potatoes with some butter and milk. It should be spreadable.
12. Use a spatula to spread the potatoes over the fish.
13. Dot with some butter, a little salt and pepper.
14. Cook in the moderate oven for 20 to 30 minutes or until the potatoes get nicely browned on top.

This dish could be garnished lightly with paprika or finely chopped parsley.

Broccoli goes very well with this comfy main course.

BENEDICT LOCKWOOD

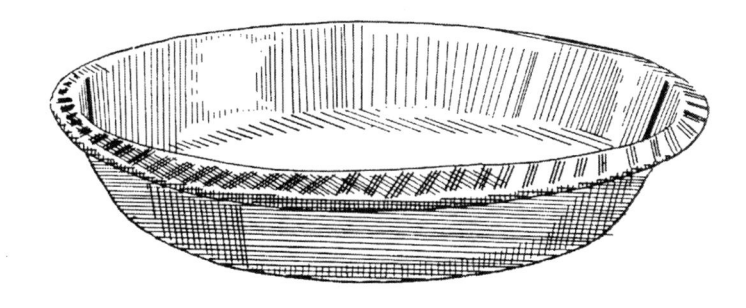

Peter Desbarats' Shrimp Dish

This recipe started about half a century ago in a restaurant on Montreal's Crescent Street. It involved a young newspaper reporter who fancied himself a cook. The other crucial participant was a real chef, a recent arrival from the Hungarian revolution. The basic ingredient was shellfish but not the shrimpy little creatures we eat these days. As the Hungarian often used to explain, scampi was something unique, a kind of super shellfish, more like lobster but even better.

He didn't have to convince the reporter. Eating scampi while listening to the adventures of his Hungarian friend was his favourite payday pastime. And the awareness of scampi's precarious future only made it more significant.

"We are the last generation that will eat shellfish," the chef would predict, "so treat it as something special."

To begin the cooking lesson, the chef would bring the reporter into his kitchen, remove the shells from increasingly rare Mediterranean scampi and dredge them with flour. Heat butter and oil in a skillet. While this was going on, the chef would break open a garlic bud and chop its contents into small bits (4 or 5 cloves). As it began to simmer in the pan, the chef would hand the reporter several ripe tomatoes and show him how to chop these into a bright red pulp.

Now the cooking would really get underway. The Hungarian chef would add the floured scampi to the pan and they would immediately start to sizzle. He would then fill a shot glass with cognac, almost to the brim, then splash it into the pan, where it quickly vapourized into a fiery globe brimming with the odours of garlic and cognac. Barely had this subsided before the reporter would dump his bowl of mashed tomato chunks into the steaming skillet, adding a quick dash of heavy cream to cool and soften the dish.

Finally a bowl of boiled rice would complete the masterpiece.

And that's the memorable recipe for scampi flambé which the young journalist would never forget and the Hungarian revolutionary would bequeath to his adopted country.

And for those of you without a friendly Hungarian chef at your side here is the more prosaic recipe:

INGREDIENTS

20 large scampi (5 per person or more to taste)
4 or 5 cloves garlic, chopped
4 or 5 large tomatoes, chopped into small mushy pieces
1/2 shot glass of cognac
2 oz butter
2 tablespoons olive oil
1/2 cup heavy cream

METHOD

1. Simmer tomatoes gently over low heat in small pan.
2. Heat butter and oil over medium heat in large frying pan and add chopped garlic, let cook for about a minute.
3. Add scampi and as they start to sizzle pour in cognac and set light to them with a match. Do this carefully and as flame dies down add tomatoes which have been cooking for a few minutes.
4. Add heavy cream and give a quick stir.

Serve immediately on bed of cooked basmati rice.

Serves 4

PETER DESBARATS

Curried Fish Dish

Fish is plentiful in Denmark and is served in all sorts of ways. Here I have flavoured it with bay leaves and curry just to give it a little exotic twist.

Ingredients

about 1-1/2 lb of cod fish fillets or other firm fish (preferably not frozen)
2 onions cut into thin round slices
6 bay leaves
2 teaspoons salt
1/2 teaspoon white pepper
2 to 3 teaspoons curry
2 to 3 tablespoons honey mustard
1-1/2 oz butter
2 tablespoons vinegar
3/4 cup cream

Method

1. Preheat oven to 350F.
2. Cut the cod fillets into serving slices and place them into a buttered baking dish.
3. Top with onions and bay leaves.
4. Melt the butter and mix well with the rest of the ingredients. If too strong add a tiny bit of sugar.
5. Pour the dressing over the fish and put the dish in the oven for about 30 minutes.

Serve with rice.
The amount of spices can be adjusted according to taste.
Serves 3 people

Ulla Troughton

Grilled Salmon Fillet

When Catherine Mallory is not working casual shifts as a registered nurse in psychiatry, she is playing violin part time with Orchestra London and The Fanshaw Chorus. Her evening suppers need to be quick, tasty and nourishing. This one fits the bill.

Equipment
Catherine prefers to use her George Foreman Grill for speed and efficiency. Those of us without this aid can adapt it to an oven grill.

Ingredients
1 large salmon fillet
1/2 teaspoon of dill seed
1 tablespoon chopped fresh parsley
juice of half a lemon
1 cup of rice.

Method
1. Preheat oven to 425F.
2. Set the rice on to cook according to package directions.
3. Mix dill seed, parsley and lemon juice.
4. Spread on the fillet.
5. Place skin side down on a grill or on a piece of foil in a hot oven.
6. Cook about eight minutes depending on the thickness of the fillet.
7. Set fillet on bed of rice.

Serves 2

Catherine Mallory

Make this recipe your own
use fresh dill
sprinkle on tamari soy
grated ginger root

Baked Trout

Fresh fish were caught in the Thames when Lord Simcoe founded this city. Colonel Talbot records grilling a trout caught in the Kettle Creek near his Lake Erie property. Today's Londoners can buy fresh trout fillets from an outdoor vendor at the Covent Garden Market or whole frozen trout from the indoor fishmonger. Rod McDowell has given us his treatment of a large trout fillet.

Ingredients
one boneless skin-on rainbow trout fillet about 12.5 oz
1 heaping tablespoon coarsely chopped capers
kosher or sea salt
coarse ground pepper
olive oil
maple syrup
zest of one lemon
parsley

Method
1. Preheat oven to 400F.
2. Place rainbow trout fillet skin side down in 9˝ by 13˝ unoiled baking dish. You could lay down a piece of foil or parchment first for easier clean-up. If it is unoiled, the fish will come away from the skin easier.
3. Lightly sprinkle with salt and ground pepper.
4. Pour a thin drizzle of your favourite olive oil the length of fillet.
5. Repeat this with the maple syrup.
6. Spread chopped capers and lemon zest along the length of fillet. If using a whole trout, smear the inside with the flavourings and spread in the capers and zest as you would a stuffing.
7. Bake uncovered for 20 minutes
8. Garnish with fresh parsley.

Serves 2 to 3

Rod McDowell

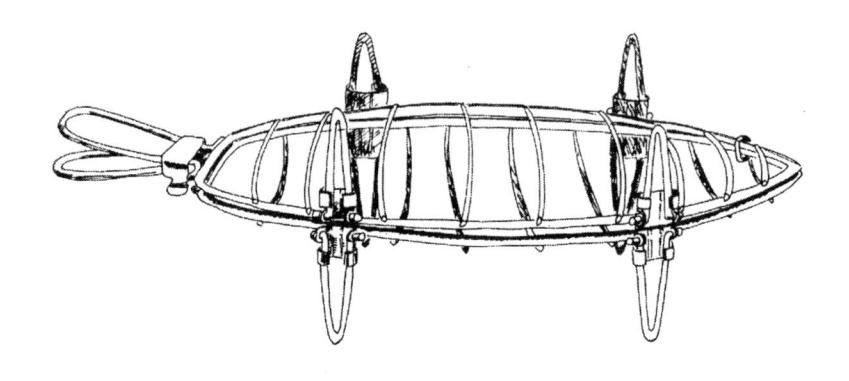

FISH AND CHIPS

Hot fish and chips wrapped in paper smell great mainly because of the vinegar. Ron McIntyre passed this secret for capturing the chip-shop flavour along to his neighbour, Ruth Hoch. The secret is to use crumbled vinegar-flavoured potato chips instead of bread crumbs. Simple but effective.

INGREDIENTS
1 bag of salt and vinegar potato chips (5 ounce will cover about 1 pound of fish.)
1 lb. of haddock, pickerel, perch or tilapia

METHOD
1. Preheat oven to 400F.
2. The easiest way to crush the chips into a bread crumb consistency is to pulse them on/off in the food processor. Failing that, pass a rolling pin over the bag several times until the desired consistency is achieved.
3. If your fish has a moist surface from being frozen, you may be able to coat it with the crumbled chips. If not, dip the fish in water or whisked egg.
4. Oil a rectangular baker with vegetable oil such as Grapeseed.
5. Bake fish at 400F for about 20 minutes, depending on the thickness of your fish.

RUTH HOCH

MAKE THIS RECIPE YOUR OWN
try different flavours of chips, such as hot or spicy varieties
serve with baked fries as on page 195
green peas are a traditional accompaniment

PRINCIPAL PLATES

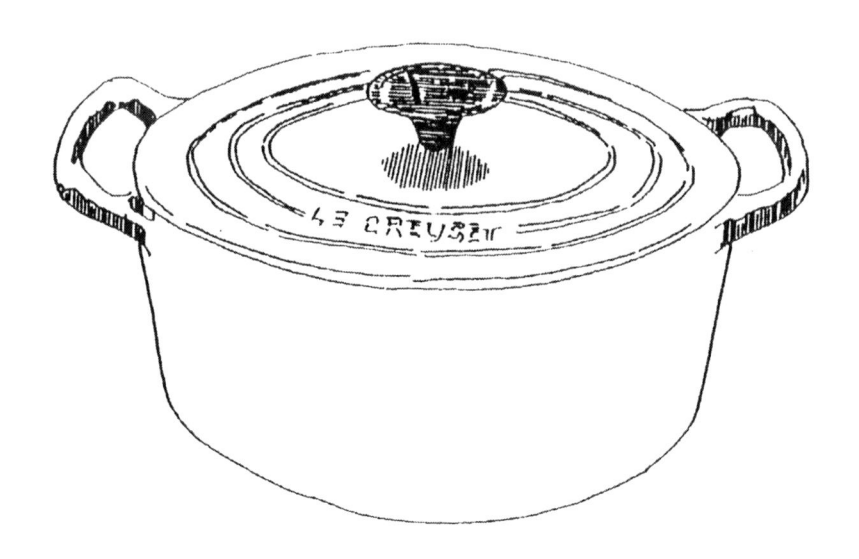

Leberli mit Rösti

This is the classic dish in Basel and the surrounding area of Baselland. Restaurants vie with each other to make the perfect dish and locals all have their favourites.

Our favourite is the Löwenzorn Restaurant in the centre of Basel. Old wooden tables and chairs and wood walls echo with the sounds of centuries of hungry Baslers.

Order Leberli and Rösti with a mixed salad with the standard Schweizer "French" Salat Sauce and some local red wine and you will be in heaven.

Rösti

For 4 servings

Start with the Rösti because it takes longer and can sit while you do the liver which must be served as soon as it is ready.

Rösti is really a Swiss hash brown. It is found all through the German part of Switzerland and is so much a part of the culture that the division between French and German Switzerland is known as the Rösti Graben. (Fried potato ditch).

Ingredients
3 medium potatoes
3 tablespoons butter
salt
milk

Method
The traditional recipe calls for boiling the potatoes the day before but I never remember to do that so this alternative works quite well.

1. Peel the potatoes then grate them using a grater with quite large holes. Wrap the grated potatoes in a clean dish towel and squeeze

as much water as you can out of them. (Rinse the dish towel well after or the starch from the potatoes will leave a stain)
2. Heat the butter in a large pan. Add the potatoes and sprinkle with salt and a little milk. With a spatula press into a round flat loaf. As soon as the potatoes start to sizzle, reduce the heat, cover and let fry undisturbed for 10 to 15 minutes.
3. Now the tricky part: with a large plate turn the Rösti over onto the plate and slide it back into the pan on the other side. Cook for another 10 to 15 minutes. Then slide it back onto the plate and sprinkle with parsley.

It should be golden brown on both sides and pale on the inside. The secret is to cook it over very low heat.
Sometimes Rösti is used as a meal in itself served with bacon and an egg on top or with cheese.

Leberli

Ingredients
28 oz calf liver or baby beef liver
4 small red onions
1/4 lb. bacon
2 oz butter
fresh ground pepper

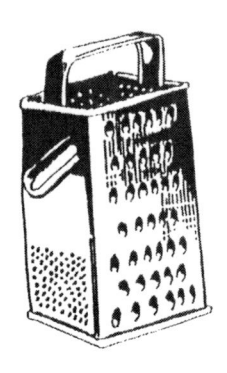

2/3 cup red wine – preferably a dark wine like Shiraz or Cabernet Sauvignon
1 tablespoon flour
1 tablespoon green peppercorns
1 tablespoon cider vinegar
1/2 teaspoon sugar
salt

Method

1. Cut liver into 3/4 inch strips. Cut bacon and onions into fine julienne.
2. Season liver strips with pepper. Heat butter in a pan and sauté liver strips on both sides.
3. Remove from the pan and keep warm.
4. Add onions and bacon to the pan and cook until the onions are golden brown.
5. Mix in 1 tablespoon flour and let cook. Add the red wine and stir gently until the sauce is rich and smooth.
6. Season with a little cider vinegar and sugar and add the peppercorns.
7. Add the liver back to the pan and serve right away. You don't want to let the liver cook anymore.

Note: do not salt the liver as it can make it tough.

Serve the Leberli with Rösti on the side on warm plates. In Basel this would be served with a Nüssli* salad and a light red wine.
En guete, bon appétit.

Nüssli also known as lamb's lettuce is only available in winter. It has a delicious nutty flavour and is usually served with a light dressing and sprinkled with crumbled hard boiled eggs.

Benedict Lockwood

Adobo Chicken

This is a very authentic dish from the Philippines which I absolutely love because it reminds me so much of my home. I remember watching my mom throwing things into a pot quite randomly.

Asking her for a recipe was a bit complicated as she never quantified her ingredients before, stating that watching her mom making the dish was simply how the information had been passed. Rather than going into details about the recipe, I have written a little poem that expresses how I feel about the dish:

When I smell that stewing pot,
That tangy, sweet and fragrant stewing pot,
I know I am home.
I smell childhood memories,
Of home-cooked meals with family,
My heritage overwhelming me,
I will cook it where I call home.
Now when I walk through my door,
Though I have walked through many doors before,
The smell of that tangy and sweet, fragrant stewing pot,
Tells me I am home.

Ingredients

- 1 whole chicken cut into pieces
- 1 cup vinegar (white or rice vinegar)
- 1/2 cup soy sauce
- 10 cloves garlic (minced)
- 2 tablespoons sugar
- 4 bay leaves

Method

1. Place the chicken and all the ingredients in a pot and mix.
2. Simmer on a medium burner for 15 minutes.
3. Add a little bit of water (1/2 cup) and simmer for 30 to 45 minutes longer until chicken is tender.
4. Serve over steamed rice. If you want to be very traditional, serve the dish with a banana.

Serves 4

Melissa Briones

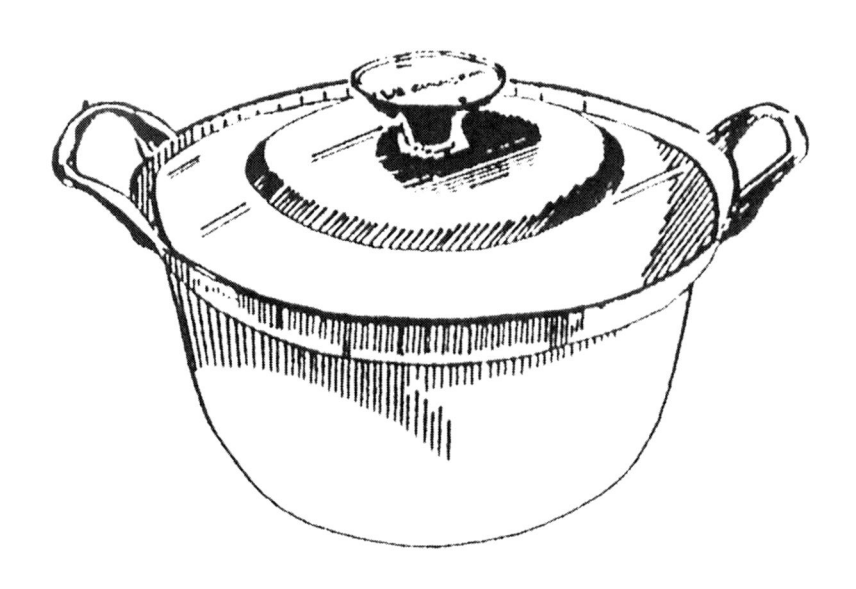

BRAISED LAMB SHANKS

Mickey Apthorp's position, director of manufacturing at Kellogg Canada Inc., keeps him focused on food products all day. He started getting involved in preparing family meals as far back as the 1970's, when the responsibility for preparing supper fell on who got home from work first.

Now he relaxes by making favourite comfort casseroles, preferably with an Italian or French twist. Lamb shanks are currently the food of the moment, but no doubt back in the early nineteenth century, Col. Thomas Talbot would have slow-simmered an iron pot of shanks (he probably called them trotters) from lambs raised on his farm. When made with veal shanks, it is called osso buco in Italy. Many of the same braising ingredients appear in both dishes.

The shanks for this recipe came from Field Gate Organics, a butcher in the Covent Garden Market, who supplies organic meat and other products.

Equipment

a heavy-based sauteuse pan with lid or large enamelled cast iron casserole

Ingredients to prepare the shanks before cooking

2 large or 4 small lamb shanks (total weight 3 to 4 lb)
enough flour seasoned with salt, pepper and herbs de provence (a finely chopped mixture of thyme, rosemary, basil, marjoram, savory) to coat the shanks
4 cloves of minced garlic
4 teaspoons olive oil
2 teaspoon chopped fresh rosemary (or half as much dried) for each shank

Ingredients to braise the lamb

2 tablespoons olive oil
1/3 cup of chopped onion
1 carrot, diced

2 cups mushroom bouillon (see supplier list)
1-1/2 cups red wine - a fruity Spanish or Portuguese
1/2 teaspoon salt
several grinds of fresh pepper
1 bay leaf
6 tablespoons tomato sauce or conserved garden tomatoes

Vegetables to be added in last hour of cooking:
1/3 cup shallots
1 cup leeks
oil and butter for sauté
2 medium carrots, sliced (try the multi-coloured ones if availible)
8 sliced Crimini mushrooms
zest of half a lemon
chopped fresh flat-leaf Italian parsley

Method

1. Preheat oven to 300F.
2. Form a paste with the garlic, olive oil and chopped rosemary.
3. Using your fingers and a sharp small knife, force this mixture between the lamb and the bone and into any available crevice. Rub oiled hands over meat surface.
4. Roll shanks in seasoned flour to coat.
5. Heat oil in large ovenproof pot.
6. Sauté the 1/3 cup of onions and diced carrot.
7. Push them to the side so that you can brown the lamb shanks on all sides.
8. Pour off any extra fat accumulated during this process.
9. Add the bouillon, wine, seasonings, tomato sauce and herbs.
10. Bring to a simmer and place it covered in the 300F oven for 1-1/2 hours, during which time you may turn and baste the shanks once.
11. Remove the shanks to a platter. Strain the sauce into another pot. Return shanks to sauce.
12. At this point the casserole may be refrigerated anywhere from 2 to 24 hours, allowing the sauce to gel, the meat to soak up flavour and the fat to rise for skimming.

13. Prepare the vegetables. Sauté the shallots and leeks gently in a small pan with a mixture of butter and oil for about 8 minutes. Toss in the sliced mushrooms for several minutes.
14. Briefly steam or blanch the sliced carrots.
15. Add the vegetables to the lamb at this point and either simmer gently on the stove or return the pot to a low oven for another half hour or until the vegetables and meat are tender.
16. Before serving, stir in the zested lemon and a handful of chopped Italian parsley.

SERVING SUGGESTIONS:

Steam some fresh green beans to present in a separate dish.
Prepare a bowl of fluffy mashed potatoes, puréed with cooked celery root or parsnip if you wish.
The Bishop's Lemon Snow (page 212) would make a refreshingly light dessert.

Serves 4

MICKEY APTHORP

Tarragon Rice with Curried Chicken

Many years ago I bought a tarragon plant at the Woodfield Plant Exchange. I wasn't sure how I would use it but thought the plant would, at least, make an attractive addition to my herb garden. It flourished and survived the winter. An old university friend passed along this recipe that makes wonderful use of the tarragon. I dry the tarragon from my garden at 421 Princess Avenue and am willing to share my harvest. The curried chicken complements the rice salad and when served cold makes a wonderful summer meal.

Ingredients

3-1/2 cups chicken stock
1-1/2 cups long grain brown or white rice (preferably basmati)
1/2 cup raisins
1/2 cup frozen peas (or cooked fresh peas)
1 teaspoon tarragon
1 garlic clove minced
2/3 cup vegetable oil
3 tablespoons good quality balsamic vinegar
salt and pepper to taste
1/2 cup green onion chopped
1/4 cup mayonnaise
Dijon mustard

Method

1. Bring chicken stock to boil and add rice. Simmer covered, for 20 to 25 minutes (a little longer for brown rice).
2. Just before all liquid is absorbed add raisins and peas and continue cooking until liquid is absorbed.
3. Combine tarragon, garlic, mustard, vegetable oil, balsamic vinegar, salt, pepper and add to rice.
4. Add chopped green onion and mayo.
5. Place in bowl in refrigerator until ready to serve.

Curried Chicken

Ingredients

6 to 8 chicken breasts, boneless and skinless
1/4 cup butter
1/2 cup honey
1/4 cup Dijon mustard
1 tablespoon curry powder or paste (mild)
2 tablespoons yellow mustard (like French's)
juice and zest of 1/2 lime
1 teaspoon salt
1 garlic clove

Method

1. Preheat oven to 350F.
2. Place chicken breasts in a 13˝ by 9˝ glass baking dish.
3. Combine the rest of the ingredients and bring to a boil.
4. Pour over chicken.
5. Bake for 45 minutes.

Serves 6. It can be served hot or cold.

Janet Dauphinee

Mild Chicken Curry

This was the first 'real' curry that I ever cooked - without pre-mixed curry powders or pastes. I was a university student in London, sharing an apartment with other students, one of whom was from India, and he taught me how he cooked his delicious mild chicken curry. I still cook this curry when I am serving dinner for friends if I don't know their tolerance of Indian spices. It is mild and tasty and a great way to introduce friends to curry if they are apprehensive of strong flavours.

All these quantities can be varied to suit your taste - but try this once just as it is, then make changes the next time. I usually add more of the aromatic spices than this recipe calls for eg: cumin and cardamom seed; chili powder can be varied considerably.

Ingredients

oil for cooking (I use coconut oil with or without the coconut flavour - it is the healthiest oil to cook with)
6 green cardamom seed pods or 1/2 teaspoon cardamom seeds
6 whole cloves
2 inch stick of cinnamon
3 cloves of garlic
5 or 6 medium onions
large pinch cumin seeds
1-1/2 teaspoons turmeric powder
1/2 teaspoon chili powder
1 teaspoon ginger (or 2 teaspoons finely chopped ginger root)
1 teaspoon salt
3 cups of plain yogurt, at room temperature
2 medium sized tomatoes chopped (if canned, drain excess juice)
3 to 4 lb or 1 whole chicken cut in pieces

Method

1. In hot oil fry cardamom, cloves, cinnamon, for a couple of minutes
2. Add cumin seeds and fry for another minute, being careful NOT to burn the spices. Remember, they are dried, and so will burn easily.
3. Add the garlic finely chopped and fry for another 30 seconds.
4. Add onions all chopped up, turn heat down to gentle, and cover. Cook till onions have sweated and the spice flavours have all come together, about 8 to 10 minutes - do not caramelize the onions.
5. Add turmeric, chili, ginger, and salt to onion mixture and cook for another minute stirring all the time - the powdered spices burn if not stirred.
6. Add tomatoes and yogurt in small amounts, for acceptance and incorporation, and stir well. A little tomato juice may be added if needed.
7. Add chicken pieces and toss thoroughly in the mixture. Fry at medium heat for a few minutes. Then turn down the heat, and simmer with a lid on until chicken is cooked, about 40 minutes.

This is generally best cooked the day ahead and re-heated for serving, since the spices have opportunity to penetrate the chicken meat.

Serve with rice and onion raita, 1-1/2 cups plain yogurt mixed with 2 chopped fresh onions, 1/2 diced peeled cucumber, juice of half a lemon, 1/2 teaspoon ground coriander seed, and 1/2 teaspoon ground cumin seed.

Hilary Moon

Born in Calcutta, Hilary spent her formative years in the North West Frontier, at the foothills of the Himalayas, in what is now Pakistan. These last years of the British Empire made her sensitive to the wide variations in seasonings found in the regions of India.

Curried Vegetables with Your Choice of Protein

Millie Hearn of Hayman Court has given us a curried vegetable base which has infinite possibilities. She has been making it for years and tried many variations. You could create a totally vegetarian meal, or add pieces of cooked beef, chicken or lamb.

Ingredients
1 small onion finely chopped
3 cloves of garlic
2 tablespoons finely sliced fresh ginger
3 tablespoons plus a separate cup of water
2 tablespoons vegetable or coconut oil
2 teaspoons curry powder (mild, medium or hot as to preference)
8 ounces mushrooms
salt

Vegetable choices - quantities dependent on your servings - limit it to three vegetables

small red potatoes	broccoli
carrots	yams
cauliflower	green beans
peas	zucchini

1/2 cup plain yogurt

Method
1. Purée the onion, garlic, ginger and 3 tablespoons of water in a blender.
2. Warm the oil in a skillet over medium heat. Cook the onion purée until most of the liquid has evaporated. (about 6 or 8 minutes).

3. Remove the stems from the mushrooms and cut them into slices. Add them to the skillet and cook 3 or 4 minutes.
4. Stir in curry powder and salt. Stir in 1 cup of water.
5. Add root vegetables first and give them about 15 minutes to simmer.
6. Green vegetables can generally be introduced for an additional 5 minutes.
7. Remove from the heat to prevent curdling when you stir in the yogurt.

MILLIE HEARN

MAKE THIS RECIPE YOUR OWN.
If you are adding some pieces of cooked meat, choose vegetables that would complement. For example - zucchini and yams with lamb, broccoli with beef, peas and cauliflower with chicken.

Piccata of Pork alla Marsala

This recipe has particular significance for John Thorp. As a young professor in Ottawa, (1980's) he signed a contract with an editor, who had travelled from Routledge Publishers in England to meet with John in Montreal, at the Chateau Champlain. In the Hotel Restaurant they dined on Piccata of Pork alla Marsala. A year later, John picked up a little booklet printed by the Catelli Pasta Company on a wire stand next to their products. It included this dish, resonant with meaning for John. The recipe was attributed to the Chef de Cuisine at the restaurant of the Chateau Champlain, 1969. John has since made it his own.

Ingredients
2 tablespoons vegetable oil
1-1/4 lb pork loin, cut into very thin slices
1 teaspoon butter
flour
1 tablespoon chopped shallots
1 tablespoon tomato paste
1/2 cup dry red wine
1 cup veal or chicken stock
1/4 cup sherry or marsala

Method
1. Salt and pepper the meat, dredge in flour, and sauté in the vegetable oil until well done.
2. Remove to serving platter. Add butter to the pan and sauté the shallots.
3. Stir in 1-1/2 tbsp flour, cooking until golden brown.
4. Add tomato paste and mix.
5. Add red wine, mix, and simmer until reduced by half.
6. Then add stock and marsala.
7. Cook for a few minutes and season to taste.

8. Pour sauce over meat.

Serve with noodles, dumplings, or spätzle.

JOHN THORP

Giant Meatballs in Caper Sauce
Koenigsberg Klopse

Kathrin Campbell makes many Woodfield women more beautiful in her professional role as an esthetician. She is also an accomplished cook, taught by her mother, Fridel, who immigrated from Germany with her husband when she was only twenty and Kathrin but a babe. Both Fridel's parents were chefs in Germany. This recipe was a staple in the family home. It is a hearty dish named after a city in East Germany, Koenigsberg. Teenage boys love it!

Ingredients
1 lb. minced beef
1 lb. minced pork
1/2 lb. minced veal
2 slightly stale buns or white bread soaked in water and squeezed dry
2 eggs
salt, pepper, chopped parsley
1 large onion
butter
4 cups chicken broth to cover
bayleaf
6 assorted colour peppercorns

Sauce ingredients
3 tablespoons butter
3 tablespoons flour
2 cups of broth
1/2 of a small jar of capers with brine
lemon juice
glass of white wine (don't drink it)
1/2 cup sour cream or creme fraiche or 35% cream

Method

1. Chop the onion into fine pieces and fry in butter until soft but not coloured.
2. Whisk the eggs with the seasonings to taste.
3. Mix meats well with beaten eggs, fried onions, and soaked bread.
4. Form into BIG meatballs - almost the size of a baseball.
5. Put into a pot with enough chicken broth to cover them.
6. Add the bay leaf and peppercorns.
7. Simmer for 30 minutes then remove the meatballs gently with a large slotted spoon.
8. Melt butter in a saucepan. Whisk in flour to make a roux or paste. Slowly beat in enough warm stock to make a gravy consistency, whisking continuously to prevent lumps.
9. Add capers with brine and a tablespoon of lemon juice.
10. Stir in a glass of white wine.
11. Stir in the cream.
12. Put meatballs in the sauce.
13. Heat gently for 15 minutes or until hot, but DO NOT BOIL.

Serve with boiled potatoes and a fresh vegetable.

Guten Appetit!

Kathrin Campbell

Pad Thai

Christine Troughton enjoys eating many Asian and South American cuisines, but Thai food is her all-time favourite. Gather friends in any season to savour this convivial dish.

Ingredients

8 oz Thai rice noodles
4 tablespoons fish sauce
4 tablespoons lime juice
4 tablespoons tomato purée (see supplier list)
2 tablespoons sugar
1 tablespoon (or more) hot red pepper flakes
1/2 cup ground peanuts
1/2 cup vegetable oil
4 cloves garlic, minced
1 lb. boneless chicken breast or thigh cut in small pieces
1 large square tofu, well drained and cut in chunks
8 very large shrimp
4 eggs, lightly beaten
4 cups bean sprouts
4 scallions (green onions), cut in half-inch pieces
Ground peanuts, lemon wedges, cucumber slices and chopped coriander for garnish.

Method

1. Soak rice noodles in cold water for 2 to 3 hours and drain just before use (or partially cook any other type of thin noodles and allow to cool).
2. Mix together fish sauce, lime juice, tomato purée, sugar and red pepper flakes; set aside.
3. Grind peanuts in food processor (at least a half cup plus extra for garnish).

4. Prepare and assemble all other ingredients.
5. In a large wok, over high heat, toss the garlic in oil.
6. Add chicken, tofu and shrimp, and sauté until lightly browned.
7. Add eggs and continue to stir-fry.
8. Add drained rice noodles and fish-sauce mixture; continue to stir-fry for about 3 minutes.
9. Add peanuts, bean sprouts and scallions, and continue to stir-fry for another 2 minutes.
10. Remove to platter.
11. Sprinkle with more ground peanuts.
12. Serve immediately with lemon wedges, cucumber slices and coriander.

Serves 4 to 6

CHRISTINE TROUGHTON

Steamed Ribs with Preserved Black Bean Sauce

Haiyun Chen has lived in Woodfield while attending Fanshawe college. He submitted this recipe in a series of photographs which illustrated the ingredients and the method. However, he does not do amounts. I have worked through it several times to give you the closest approximation to his intent. The results have been very tasty.

Equipment

Improvise a steamer by setting a heatproof bowl (stainless steel would work) on a rack in a large pan which can be covered. An oriental vegetable cleaver is very handy for dicing and chopping.

Ingredients

- 4 one inch strips of pork ribs
- 2 tablespoons of black beans preserved in garlic (see supplier list at the back of the book)
- 2 tablespoons finely chopped fresh ginger root
- 1 teaspoon white peppercorns
- 3 teaspoons dark soya sauce
- 3 teaspoons light soya sauce
- 1/2 teaspoon of sugar or 2 teaspoons of honey
- 2 teaspoons of cornstarch
- 2 tablespoons peanut oil

Method

1. Cut the ribs between the bone into single pieces.
2. Peel the ginger and chop into fine pieces.
3. Crush the dried white peppercorns or use a pepper grinder.
4. Chop the preserved black beans.
5. Mix the minced ginger, white pepper and black beans in the bowl.
6. Add the rib pieces to the bowl with the soya sauces, oil, sugar, and

cornstarch.
7. Marinate for 15 minutes.
8. Place the rack in the pot with water under it. Bring to a boil.
9. Set the bowl with the rib mixture on the rack.
10. Cover and steam for 20 to 25 minutes.

HAIYUN CHEN

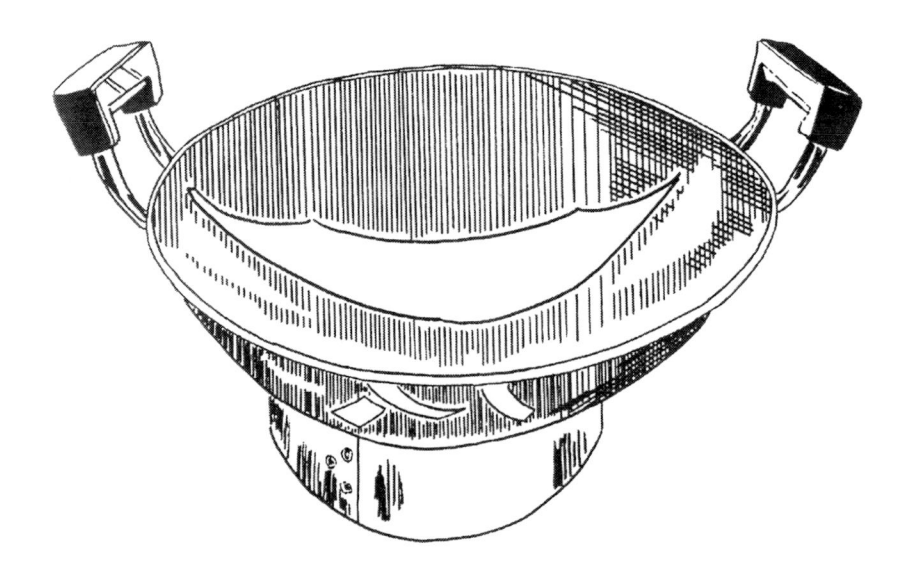

Peggy's Glazed Spareribs

The Rib Fest is one of London's popular summer festivals, held in Victoria Park, the entrance to Woodfield. Buy a ticket, line up at a couple of the smoking, fragrant BBQ pits and make your choice. Peggy Curnoe's family made their decision thirty years ago. Husband Glen cast his vote in their kitchen for her glazed spareribs, made with a secret sauce which she is now sharing with you.

Equipment
a shallow metal roasting pan lined with foil for easy cleaning

Ingredients
5 lbs of ribs (allow 2 to 3 spareribs per person)
1 tablespoon of grated fresh ginger root
2 cloves of crushed garlic
3 tablespoons of ketchup
4 tablespoons of molasses
2 tablespoons of soy sauce
2 tablespoons of lemon juice

Method
1. Preheat oven to 350F degrees.
2. Cut the ribs into 1 inch sections. Peggy uses the big ribs and trims off any excess fat prior to cooking
3. Toss the cut ribs in the pan with grated ginger and crushed garlic.
4. Bake in the oven uncovered for 40 minutes.
5. Prepare the sauce by mixing together ketchup, molasses, soy and lemon.
6. Reduce heat to 300F.
7. Pour off fat that has accumulated in the pan.
8. Add the sauce and mix thoroughly to coat all of the ribs.
9. Return to oven for 35 minutes at the lower temperature.

10. During the remainder of the cooking time, stir to distribute sauce evenly over ribs.
11. Serve at once when ribs are crisp and well glazed.

PEGGY CURNOE

An Indonesian Buffet at the Arnolds

Peter and Irene are the proud owners of one of Woodfield's handsome Victorian homes, which they keep filled with friends and a large family. The dining room table is often spread for a buffet, including these three dishes, favourites in the Arnold household.

These recipes were given to Irene years ago by an Austrian friend who was married to a Dutch man, both accomplished cooks. She has brought them to our Harvestfest Pot Lucks.

Indonesian Rice

Equipment
A sauté pan 10" to 12" wide, a large fry pan with deep straight sides, would be handy.

Ingredients
2 cups of basmati rice
1 large onion, finely chopped
2 leeks, chopped
1 cup of chopped carrots
1-1/2 lbs. of ground veal or pork
Ketjap Manis (Indonesian sweet soya sauce)
Nasi Goreng (see supplier list at back of book for these seasonings)
Sambal Oelek (hot chili paste)

Method
1. Cook the rice in 4 cups of water with 1 teaspoon salt for about 25 minutes.
2. Soak the Nasi mix in hot water.
3. Sauté the chopped onion, leeks, carrots and ground meats in a large deep-sided frypan or sauté pan.
4. Add the soaked Nasi.
5. Mix cooked rice into the vegetable and meat mixture. You may

need to transfer to a large bowl.
6. Add sambal and ketjap to taste.

Pork with Peanut Butter Sauce

Ingredients
2 pork tenderloins cut in 1 inch pieces
1 tablespoon cornstarch
1 tablespoon curry powder
2 tablespoons Ketjap Manis
3 tablespoons peanut oil

Ingredients for Sauce
1 cup chunky peanut butter
1 teaspoon Sambal Oelek
1 tablespoon Ketjap Manis

Method
1. Toss the pieces of pork tenderloin in a mixture of cornstarch, curry powder, and Ketjap. Allow it to marinate for at least 30 minutes.
2. Combine peanut butter, Sambal and Ketjap in a saucepan on low heat.
3. Add enough boiling water to make a thick sauce.
4. Stir over low heat until amalgamated.
5. Fry pork on both sides in hot oil.
6. Place pork on a platter. Pour sauce over.

Cucumber Salad

Irene recommends that you offer this refreshing salad with the above dishes.

Ingredients
1 English cucumber, sliced
1 clove of minced garlic
1/4 cup of chopped fresh dill
2 tablespoons white vinegar

6 tablespoons vegetable oil
salt, pepper and a smidge of sugar to taste

METHOD
1. Place the cucumber in a bowl.
2. Whisk or shake the remaining ingredients to make the dressing.
3. Toss the sliced cucumbers in the dressing.

IRENE SAY

Meat Rolls or Rouladen

I came to Canada from Germany when I was nearly fifteen and my mother continued to cook the food she had always cooked, even though it was sometimes difficult to get the ingredients. Once I got maried I wanted to make some of the family dishes but realized I had no idea how, so my mother sent me her recipes. One of these was for rouladen.

Ingredients

Per Person:
- 1 thin, vaguely rectangular slice of round steak (purchased from a butcher)
- 1 pickle
- 1 or 2 slices of bacon
- paprika
- salt
- tomato paste
- mustard
- water or red wine
- oil for sautéing

Method

1. Sprinkle each slice with paprika and salt.
2. Spread tomato paste and mustard on meat.
3. Place 1 or 2 slices of bacon over top.
4. Roll the meat tightly around a pickle nearly as wide as the meat, and fasten with toothpicks.
5. Sauté the rolls in enough oil, so that they are nicely browned on all sides. Don't hurry this, since the flavour of the sauce depends on it.
6. Add 1-1/2 cup water or red wine for 6 rolls.
7. Simmer covered for 1 hour and 15 minutes, until quite soft.

You can thicken the gravy with flour or more tomato paste if you like

Regina Moorcroft

Boeuf Daube Niçoise avec Gnocchi

Thanks to web magic, we located an apartment in an eighteenth-century block, in the historic centre of Nice, surrounded by all that gives value to life. The precariously small balcony hung over Le Cours Saleya, four long rows of vendors' stalls loaded with olives and lavender from the hills that hug the bay and glistening with fish from its waters. Jewel-toned fruits and vegetables from Spain and Africa fill baskets under striped awnings that run parallel to palms fringing the Mediterranean.

The location's icing on the cake was Bar de la Terrasse, the small brasserie that anchors the key corner of the block. Every morning their chalkboard straddled the sidewalk announcing the chef's daily special plate. The most memorable was daube Niçoise avec gnocchi. Chunks of beef that fell apart on the fork in a dark, spicy sauce with a hint of orange, so good I asked for a take-away for David. While the waiter brought me a complimentary espresso, the chef scraped all that was left of the day's special into a large white bowl for me to carry upstairs. The bartender willingly wrote the name of the cut of beef used on the back of my bill. Joue - beef cheek, or jarret, best translated as rump. The method and ingredients are similar to the classic Boeuf Bourguigon, with the following exceptions that give the dish a regional Provençal flavour. The waiter helped me with preparation tips in his broken English and my fractured French.

Equipment
a large cast iron enamelled Dutch oven

Ingredients
To serve eight.
3 lb. rump roast
olive oil for browning meat
4 cups of gnocchi
a piece of pork rind or belly
1 tablespoon tomato paste

1 cup rich beef broth
1 cup Niçoise olives
1 orange
3 carrots
parsley, salt, pepper
a little cornstarch or flour may be used for thickening sauce

Marinade

2 onions, chopped
1 stalk celery, chopped
2 carrots, sliced
olive oil
2 cloves of garlic, crushed
1 bottle of full-bodied red wine
a bouquet garni, in a muslin bag - branches of fresh thyme, parsley, 10 black peppercorns, a bay leaf
2 or 3 strips of thick orange rind

Method

1. Sauté onions, celery, carrots until soft in the olive oil in a large Dutch oven.
2. Add garlic, herbs, wine and strips of orange rind.
3. Simmer for 20 minutes. Cool.
4. Cut beef into large 2 inch chunks.
5. Add it to the pot of marinade ingredients.
6. If beef is not covered, add more wine.
7. Cover and refrigerate overnight. Stir at least once.

Preparation

1. When ready to cook, heat oven to 250F.
2. Remove the beef and dry it on paper towels.
3. Strain the marinade, reserving the liquid, discard the solids.
4. Cover the bottom of the Dutch oven in a film of olive oil. Heat to medium.
5. Brown the beef chunks in two batches if necessary.
6. Deglaze the pot with beef broth and any juices which have accu-

mulated on the platter of beef.
7. Return the beef and chunk of pork to the pan.
8. Add strained marinade with a few more fresh orange strips.
9. Bring to a simmer on top of the stove.
10. Put into a low oven for three hours.
11. At this point you could cool overnight, skim off the fat and reheat for the finishing steps of this dish.

Finishing the Sauce
---
1. Bring pot back to a simmer.
2. Stir in the tomato paste.
3. Peel and slice 3 carrots.
4. Cook gently with the sauce and beef.
5. Stir in the Niçoise olives.
6. If the sauce is not thick enough, blend in a tablespoon of cornstarch or flour blended with 1/4 cup cold water.
7. Season with salt and ground pepper.
8. Serve beside boiled gnocchi with a garnish of parsley.

Ann Lindsay

Tajine aux Poires et au Miel

Our closest friends in France, Michel and Nancy Janon, are actually "pieds noirs", that is, of French ancestry, but born and raised in Algeria (nobody knows for sure how the epithet "black feet" got applied to the French colonists there). They are both fabulous cooks, full of verve to experiment and explore. But the cuisine that is most natural to them is that of their birth and childhood, the cuisine of Algeria. I remember Nancy taking down her mother's hand-written recipe book to copy out this recipe for us. It is the genuine article: no fusion here!

Ingredients
2 lbs shoulder of lamb or leg of lamb
1 lb firm pears (Bosc)
2 tablespoons olive oil
1 teaspoon (or more to taste) ginger powder
1 good pinch saffron
1 onion (whole)
1 bouquet fresh coriander
salt and pepper to taste
1 teaspoon cinnamon powder
honey
rosewater

Method
1. Heat oil in saucepan
2. While oil is heating cut lamb into 1 inch pieces and remove any fat.
3. Brown the meat in the hot oil in several batches, removing the browned meat as it is ready and reserve until all the meat is brown.
4. Return the meat to the pan and add the ginger, saffron, salt, onion, and coriander. Cover with water and simmer until the meat is tender and the liquid is reduced to a thick sauce.

5. Remove the onion and the coriander.
6. While meat is cooking, peel, quarter and pit the pears and stew them gently until tender/firm, then add them to the lamb.
7. Drizzle with honey and rosewater.

Serve on a bed of cooked couscous and, if you like, delay drizzling of honey and sprinkling of rosewater until serving time.

Serves 4

JOHN THORP

Steak and Kidney Pie

This dish appears in Mrs. Beeton's "Every Day Cookery and Housekeeping Book", revised edition, published in England in 1890 and it has remained a constant in British cuisine. My version has evolved over the years to the following.

Equipment
heavy pot to cook steak and kidney mixture
oval or oblong pie dish with border to take pastry
china pie bird or pie funnel

Ingredients
1-1/2 lbs of flank steak or good quality stewing beef cut in 1 inch cubes
flour for dredging meat and kidney
2 oz. coconut oil or butter
4 oz. veal kidney cut into small pieces
1 medium onion chopped
6 mushrooms cut into small pieces (use stalks as well)
2 cups beef stock or water or mixture of both
salt and pepper
pastry for pie (see recipe below)
1/2 beaten egg to brush on finished pie before cooking

Method
1. Heat coconut oil or butter in heavy stewing pan.
2. Dredge the meat and kidney with flour and salt and pepper to taste.
3. Brown the above over medium high heat in single layer batches (several minutes each) and remove to plate or bowl.
4. Add the onion to the remaining fat and cook for a few minutes until tender but not brown.
5. Add the mushrooms and cook a few minutes more.

6. Return meat mixture to pan and add the stock mixture.
7. Bring to a boil and simmer for an hour and a half until meat is tender.
8. Add a little more salt and pepper if necessary.
9. Let the above mixture cool while making pastry or alternatively refrigerate until next day and then add pastry. (I find it better the next day).

Pastry

This recipe was given to me by my roommate when I was waiting for my eldest daughter to be born – a very long time ago. It may bear a striking resemblance to the recipe on the Tenderflake lard package but I prefer to associate it with Jenny's birth. The recipe makes enough pastry for three double crust pies.

Ingredients
1 lb lard
5 cups all purpose flour
1 teaspoon salt
1 teaspoon baking powder
2 teaspoons icing sugar (optional)
1 egg
1 tablespoon vinegar
water

Method
1. Preheat oven to 400F.
2. Sift together flour, salt, baking powder and icing sugar.
3. Lightly beat egg in a 1 cup measuring glass and add the vinegar and the water to 1 cup level.
4. Add lard cut in large chunks to flour and rub in with fingertips until like breadcrumbs.
5. Add liquid mixture a little at a time until it holds together (probably 1/2 cup).
6. Knead VERY lightly into one ball or oblong and cut off enough

for pie crust. (The rest can be divided into several patties, wrapped in wax paper and placed in plastic or wax paper bag in freezer for future use).
7. Roll out pastry and cut 1-1/2" strip to cover around border and press down all the way round.
8. Roll remaining pastry to a couple of inches bigger than pie dish.
9. Place meat mixture in pie dish and place pie bird or funnel in the middle of it. Kind of measure where pie funnel is and cut a cross in pastry so that pastry cover will slide over it.
10. Place pastry cover over dish - press down all the way around... mark with fork as decoration and trim any overhang. You can cut out a few shapes and decorate pie if you wish.
11. Brush pastry with egg mixture (optional) for a shiny crust.
12. Bake in 400F. oven for 25 to 30 minutes until pastry is golden brown.

Serve immediately with boiled potatoes and green vegetable.

HAZEL DESBARATS

Irish Beef Stew

When Gabriele Sanio was a twelve year-old student at Lorne Avenue School, her mother taught her how to prepare this basic family meal before she returned to Germany for four weeks and left her to make it for her brothers. Now she makes big pots of stews for the International Students from University of Western who home-stay with her family in Woodfield. One pot meals are essential because of her full professional work schedule.

She teaches several courses on landscape design at Fanshawe College and delivers spring and fall seminars at Lee Valley on residential garden design and maintenance. Seven Woodfield gardens have had "Gabby Makeovers". As project leader for Reforest London, she co-ordinates the planting of trees for reading circles on school lawns.

In her spare time, she sends monthly garden articles to an Irish magazine and grows the carrots, onions and potatoes for this stew in her plot at the Community Gardens.

Equipment
Gabriele uses a pressure cooker but a heavy Dutch oven works just as well, as would a slow cooker.

Ingredients
1-1/2 lb. piece of blade roast or short rib roast
2 slices of bacon
1 medium onion
3 large potatoes
4 medium carrots
1/2 small turnip
3 cups beef bouillon
2 teaspoons cornstarch
salt and pepper to taste

chopped fresh parsley

Method

1. Cut bacon into one inch pieces and fry gently in a cast iron or heavy-based dutch oven.
2. Trim excess fat and sinews from the meat. Cut it into one inch cubes.
3. Brown with the bacon in its fat.
4. Add chopped onion and cook until it is translucent.
5. Cover with beef broth (see supplier list) and simmer gently for about an hour either on the stove or in a low 250F oven.
6. Scrub and/or peel the potatoes, carrots and turnip. Cut into one inch cubes. Add to meat cubes when they are almost tender.
7. Continue cooking on a low heat until vegetables are done. (about 30 to 40 minutes)
8. Blend cornstarch with 1/4 cup of water and stir in to thicken the sauce.
9. Season to taste with salt, pepper and perhaps some chopped parsley.

Gabriele suggests serving this with freshly blanched green beans.

Gabriele Sanio

A Steak by Any Other Name

Flank steak is a long, thin piece of meat cut from the side of the cow. Although inexpensive it is tasty if treated right. Most serious food writers have offered a recipe for marinating then grilling this lean piece of flank. It is easy to prepare and open to a variety of seasoning. James Beard's is the simplest. He instructs us to remove the tough membranes on the outside, flash it under a hot broiler for five minutes a side, sprinkle with salt and pepper, then slice thinly on the diagonal. Thirty years ago, Craig Claiborne of the New York Times, rubbed the meat with garlic, brushed it with salad oil and called it London Broil.

The marinade ingredients have changed with the tastes of each generation, as has the name given to this dish, but the cooking procedure has stayed fairly constant.

Equipment
A very sharp knife is essential.
You need a rectangular glass dish for marinating, as acidic ingredients can corrode metal.

Method to follow for any of the following options
1. Cut off any white membrane or fat from the meat.
2. Score the surface with a cross-hatch pattern.
3. Combine the marinade ingredients and pour them over the meat in a shallow glass dish.
4. Marinate in the refrigerator for up to 24 hours, turning it over occasionally.
5. Heat the grill or broiler.
6. Remove meat from marinade.
7. Broil or grill for up to 5 minutes a side.
8. Let meat rest for 10 minutes before slicing on the diagonal into thin slices.

Here is a sampling of marinade suggestions from Woodfield Flank Steak enthusiasts.

Flank Steak Teriyaki from Ruth Hoch

This recipe came from a colleague at the health unit. I have made it hundreds of times. It is great for serving a crowd at the cottage and the leftovers make perfect baguette sandwiches or an addition to stir fries.

Ingredients
1-1/2 lbs. flank steak
1/2 cup soy sauce
2 tablespoons brown sugar
2 tablespoons worchestershire sauce
1 tablespoon vinegar
1/2 teaspoon ginger (or 1 tablespoon freshly grated ginger)
1 garlic clove, minced

Angie Killoran's Marinade Inspiration

Angie Killoran's marinade inspiration, from an old Julia Child television cooking show, quickly became her teenage sons' favourite:

Ingredients
a bunch of green onions finely minced - split the onion lengthwise before chopping
1/2 cup of light tamari sauce which has less salt and more flavour than regular soy
4 tablespoons of fresh lemon juice
4 tablespoons of olive oil

John Thorp's Asian Grilled Steak

John Thorp introduces some heat to the marinade and suggests serving the thin slices on a bed of greens.

Ingredients
1/2 bunch cilantro, including roots, stems, leaves
2 cloves garlic, chopped
1 tablespoon chopped ginger root
1 teaspoon hot chili paste
2 tablespoons hoisin sauce
2 tablespoons soy sauce
2 tablespoons lemon juice
1 lb flank steak prepared as in the method given above

Today's popularity of fajitas have us squeezing lime juice on the steak and chopping fresh cilantro with jalepeno peppers for a Latin hit. Flank Steak/London Broil/ Teriyaki/ Asian Steak/Salsa Steak. Dance to your own beat. Any Zumba Steak recipes out there?

SIDES AND SAUCES

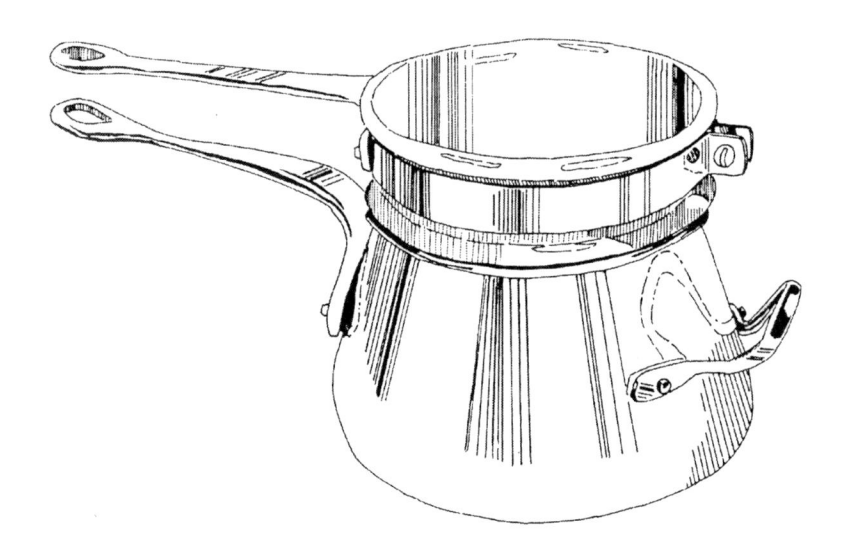

A Selection of Recipes from the Hayman Apartments

London's first apartment building, the Victoria, was built in 1908 on Queens Avenue by John and Will Hayman. In the next few years, an attractive complex of three and four storey red brick apartment buildings developed on the block bounded by Queens, Wellington, Dufferin and Picton Streets. The interiors were spacious, with appointments, such as elegant fireplaces, high cornice ceilings, and generous bowed windows. London's presidents of corporations, politicians and professionals moved in to become part of this trend-setting new life style in the centre of the city.

In 1985, new owners Decade Development, announced plans to completely renovate the apartments while maintaining the gracious exteriors and many of the fine interior appointments.

Now these quality spaces attract a new clientele that is representative of the vibrant face of our city.

Tianbing, Traditional Chinese Pancakes

Hong Chen-DeCloet lives in a condominium in Hayman Court. She immigrated to Canada eight years ago and works as an interpreter/translator here in London. This traditional Chinese recipe comes from her mother.

Ingredients
1 cup of white wheat flour
2-1/2 cups of water
2 eggs
1/4 chopped onion
1 teaspoon of table salt

cooking oil - peanut or sunflower

Method
1. Whisk egg with water.
2. Make batter by gradually whipping water and egg into the flour.
3. Mix in chopped onion and salt.
4. Heat 2 teaspoons of cooking oil in a frying pan swirling it around to cover evenly.
5. Ladle a scoop of batter into the centre of the pan and rotate so that it forms a round shape.
6. Return the pan to the burner until one side solidifies. Flip to the other side.
7. Remove to a plate and continue with the rest of the batter, adjusting heat and adding more oil.

We eat these savoury pancakes with various sauces, such as Thai Sweet Chili Sauce, some pieces of pork or chicken stir fried.

Hong Chen-DeCloet

Recipes from Vintage Apartments

Riva and Al Ellinson have been Woodfield apartment dwellers for almost five decades. When they immigrated from Britain in the 1950's, they moved into Mountbatten House on Central Avenue. From 1963 to 1985 they lived in the Hayman apartments on Queens Avenue near Picton Street. The next ten years were spent in The Four Seasons Apartments at the corner of Queens and Colborne Streets. They are exemplary core residents. Their children attended Lord Roberts and Central Highschool and they operated the memorable gift store, Serendipity, in downtown London for forty years. Riva associates her time in The Hayman with memories of two people very dear to her. She is sharing them through their recipes.

Gracie's Roast Potatoes

As a war-widow in Bournemouth, Gracie perfected roasting potatoes for lodgers in her home during the summer holidays. During the eighteen years she lived with Al and Riva in the Hayman building, the Sunday roast was always accompanied by perfectly crisped roast potatoes.

Ingredients
enough potatoes for the family meal
enough lard to roast the potatoes

Method
1. Peel and half the potatoes.
2. Par-boil in salted water for 3 to 5 minutes.
3. Melt the lard around the roast (meat or poultry) in a 350F oven.
4. Arrange the potatoes in the pan.
5. Bake approximately one hour, turning frequently to prevent sticking.

6. After removing the roast, drain excess fat leaving potatoes in to crisp if they have not already done so. Or you may transfer them to a non-stick pan with a little of the fat to speed up the process. You want a crunchy exterior and wonderfully soft interior.

Riva always had first choice for the crispiest.

RIVA ELLINSON

If you want to make the perfect Yorkshire Pudding to accompany the roast and potatoes, cellist Julia MacGregor, recommends Delia Smith's recipe in her "Complete Cookery Course.".

Curried Mayonnaise

Jim Cooke walked all over London giving piano lessons to young and old. Many of his students repeated their sessions with Jim just to enjoy his vibrant personality and his brandy laced coffee, served after class in a small downtown studio. Jim lived for a while in the Centennial House Apartments, very near the Ellinsons. They recall him climbing up the four floors of the Hayman apartments, booming out greetings on every landing. He brought back many recipes from his travels in Europe, including this versatile dip/sauce.

Ingredients
1 cup mayonnaise
1 teaspoon of curry powder
1/4 teaspoon of ginger
1/2 small clove of garlic minced (double this if you like)
2 green onions (scallions) minced
1-1/2 tablespoons of liquid honey

Method
Blend together at high speed in a blender or processor.

This is an excellent dip for crudities or sauce to accompany poached salmon or steamed asparagus.

Jim Cooke

Red Cabbage

This is my mother's recipe and an integral part of our Christmas dinner, mostly because it's so much trouble, that Christmas is the only time I make it.

Equipment
1 large pot

Ingredients
1 medium red cabbage shredded
4 or more peeled, quartered apples, soft ones like golden delicious. You should have the same quantity of apples as cabbage.
1 medium minced onion
4 tablespoons cider vinegar
2 tablespoons sugar
2 bacon slices, chopped
1/4 teaspoon ground cloves
3 tablespoons red currant jelly
2 tablespoons flour
salt

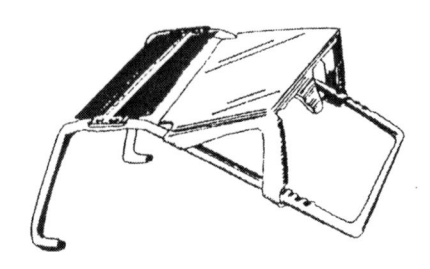

METHOD

1. Layer shredded cabbage, apples and onions in the pot and salt each layer using a salt shaker.
2. Add water until you can just see it through the top of the cabbage
3. Add all other ingredients except jelly and flour and simmer for several hours.
4. Uncover the pot and watch until water is nearly gone.
5. Add jelly, sprinkle flour over top and stir. Boil for a minute before serving.

REGINA MOORCROFT

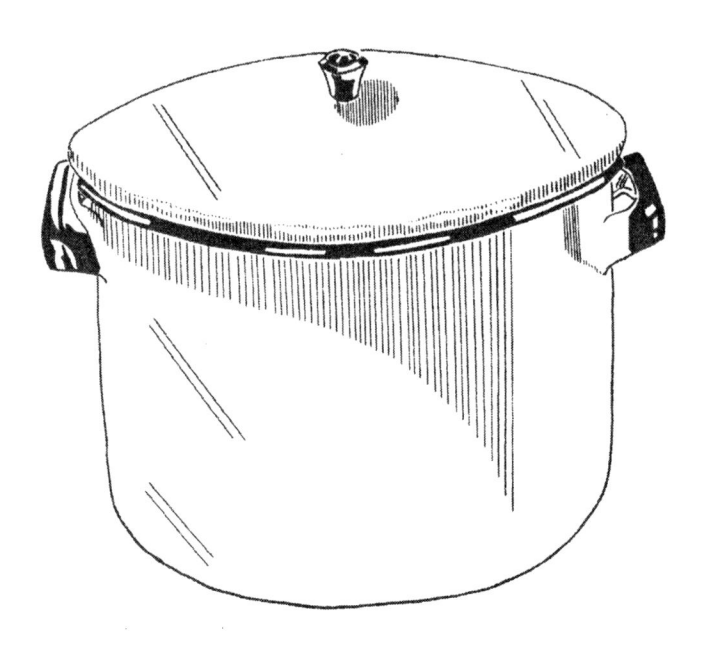

Mushroom Loaf

This is a versatile recipe which you can use as a stuffing for fowl, an appetizer spread or a side accompaniment to roast meats. It was passed along to me by a friend who has a French Canadian background.

Ingredients

3 tablespoon butter, melted
1 onion chopped finely
1 garlic bud, minced
1 stalk of chopped celery
1 lb. of mushrooms trimmed and chopped
2 cups of breadcrumbs
Salt and pepper to taste
2 tablespoons minced parsley
1 egg

Method

1. Preheat oven to 375F
2. Sauté chopped onion, garlic and celery in the melted butter until soft.
3. Add prepared mushrooms.
4. Blend the breadcrumbs into this mixture.
5. Add seasonings and parsley to taste.
6. Pack the mixture into a small greased loaf pan.
7. Beat the egg with 1/2 cup of water and pour over the top.
8. Bake for 25 to 30 minutes.

If you are intending to use this as a tasty stuffing for game birds or chicken, use chicken stock in place of the water and add sage or poultry seasonings.

Peggy Curnoe

Cumberland Sauce

Lorraine de Blois has a sour cherry tree and a gooseberry bush in her front yard on Prospect Avenue. She uses the fruit to make a sour cherry gooseberry jam. In her back yard she has red currant bushes which she harvests for red currant jelly. The slow food movement is alive and well in the heart of Woodfield.

The red currant jelly is a chief ingredient in her Cumberland sauce, an ideal accompaniment for ham and scalloped potatoes.

Ingredients
rind and juice of 2 oranges
rind and juice of 1 lemon
8 oz of red currant jelly
1 cup of port
1/2 teaspoon of powdered ginger
large pinch of cayenne
salt to taste

Method
1. Pare rinds with peeler or citrus zester.
2. Cut into thin matchstick strips.
3. Blanch in small pan of water for 5 minutes.
4. Drain and set aside.
5. Melt jelly.
6. Add port, orange and lemon juices, spices and salt.
7. Boil for 15 minutes.
8. Add blanched peel.
9. Can be served warm or cold.

This is the definitive sauce to accompany game, such as venison or duck.

Lorraine de Blois

A Selection of Sides

Herb Rice

Ingredients
1/2 cup of wild rice
1 cup (or as directed on package) vegetable or chicken stock
1 clove garlic, minced
1 handful of fresh herbs of your choice (cilantro, oregano, rosemary)
1 tablespoon olive oil
1 onion, diced

Method
1. In a heavy pot, heat olive oil.
2. Sauté garlic and onion until fragrant and onion is softened.
3. Pour stock into pot then rice. Bring to boil then simmer on low (as directed), covered.
4. When the rice is cooked, add the herbs, stir and let sit for five minutes to allow flavours to develop.

To Die For Mashed Potatoes

My mother always made the best mashed potatoes and a little while ago I asked her what she added to them to make them so tasty. It is so simple I ask myself, "Why didn't I think of that?"

Ingredients
baking potatoes, peeled and cut (number depends on how many hungry mouths to feed)
1 teaspoon salt
2 tablespoons butter or margarine
about 1/4 cup buttermilk (in place of milk)

Method

1. Boil potatoes until tender.
2. Mash with potato masher. Add salt, butter and buttermilk and whip until smooth and creamy.

Homemade French Fries

Cut up 4 or 5 whole baking potatoes or sweet potatoes lengthwise into finger sizes. Drip some olive oil over to coat potatoes. Place on a baking sheet and sprinkle with a little sea salt or other seasoning. Bake for 20 to 30 minutes in the oven at 350 F.

Kristen Gaudet

Eat Your Greens

We grow them, we buy them, we know they are good for us....but how do we make them interesting? Here are a few suggestions.

Brilliant Broccoli

Equipment
a 10 inch sauté pan with cover

Ingredients
1 onion
2 tablespoons olive oil
1 tablespoon soy sauce diluted in a little water
2 tablespoons sesame seeds
1 tablespoon sesame oil
1 head of broccoli

Method
1. Lightly toast the sesame seeds in a little sesame oil. Be careful not to let them brown. Set aside.
2. Slice the onion thinly. Lightly fry in the olive oil.
3. Add broccoli spears and stir fry for a couple of minutes.
4. Pour in the soy sauce and water.
5. Cover and steam gently for five minutes.
6. Sprinkle with the sesame seeds and a little warm sesame oil.

Benedict Lockwood

Maple Walnut Brussel Sprouts

Bonnie MacLachlan and John Thorp have made this dish a feature of their Christmas dinner.

Ingredients

4 cups of brussel sprouts
4 tablespoons sherry vinegar
4 tablespoons pure maple syrup
1 tablespoon Dijon mustard
1/2 cup walnut oil
pinch of freshly grated nutmeg
salt and freshly ground black pepper
1 cup coarsely chopped walnuts

Method

1. Steam the sprouts.
2. Meanwhile, whisk the vinegar, maple syrup and mustard together.
3. Gradually whisk in the oil.
4. Season with nutmeg, salt and pepper.
5. Toss the hot brussel sprouts with the walnuts and the vinaigrette.

John Thorp

Conserving Tomatoes

Even cooks who are conscientious about using fresh produce keep cans of tomatoes on their pantry shelves in the winter months. They know that fresh ones are tasteless out of season. Here is a very simple method for conserving the bushels of luscious Ontario tomatoes in our fall markets for later use. This procedure was first printed in 1806 in an early cookery book by Mrs. Rundell, entitled A New System of Domestic Cookery. It was revived thirty years ago by Elizabeth David.

Equipment
A cast iron enamelled dutch oven. It must be coated or the acid in the tomatoes with draw out rust. An earthenware or porcelain casserole would also work, preferably large enough to hold about four quarts of tomatoes.
A food mill fitted with a medium disc is essential.

Ingredients
Enough fresh tomatoes to fill your oven pot of choice. Plum tomatoes are best for reducing as they have more pulp.

Method
1. Heat oven to 350F.
2. Wash the tomatoes and pack them into your pot. Do not peel, core or cut them unless you are removing a blemish.
3. Cover with a proper fitting lid and leave in the moderate oven for about an hour.
4. Remove when the tomatoes are a thoroughly softened mass.
5. Drain off any excess clear liquid.
6. Fit the food mill over a bowl large enough to receive the resulting sauce.
7. Ladle the stewed tomatoes into the mill. Turn until all are squeezed through. The skin and seeds are held back by the disc

and you have a purée.
8. At this point, I put it into plastic containers of convenient size and freeze them to be doctored according to future use.
9. You can season by simmering with garlic and herbs or shallots according to your recipe requirements.

ANN LINDSAY

DESSERTS

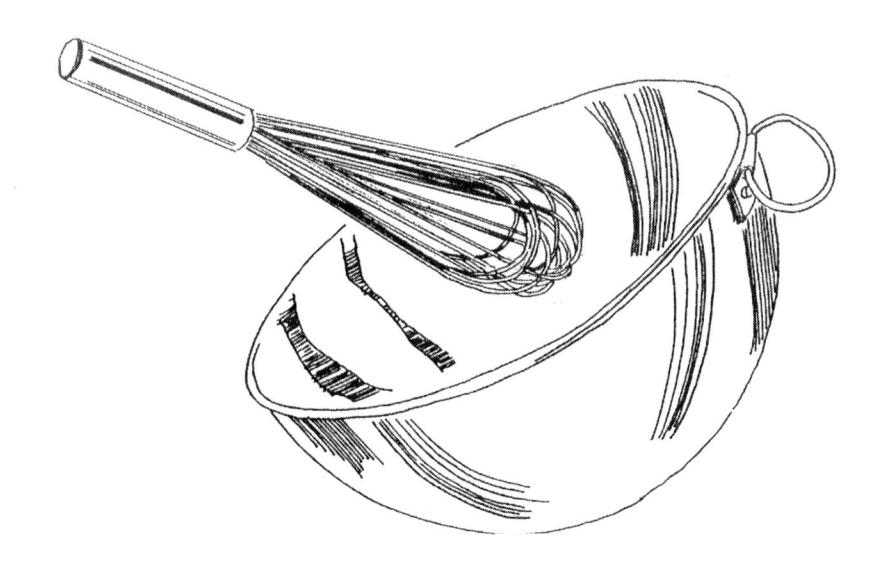

Mocha Torte

Alice Thomson lives in one of the condominiums of Queens Court, one of the original Hayman buildings on Wellington Street. This dramatic confection has become her family's favourite for birthday celebrations.

Ingredients

1 large angel food cake (preferably a day old to make slicing easier)
1/2 pound of butter
1-1/2 cup sifted icing sugar
pinch of salt
1 teaspoon vanilla
2 egg yolks
2 egg whites
2 squares unsweetened chocolate
6 tablespoons double strength coffee
1 cup of whipping cream
1 teaspoon vanilla
preserved ginger or other garnish

Method

1. Using a long, sharp carving knife, slice the cake across into 5 slices making four layers.
2. Cream the butter.
3. Gradually add the sifted icing sugar, beating until smooth.
4. Add salt, vanilla and 2 egg yolks. Beat thoroughly.
5. Melt the chocolate over hot water.
6. Blend the chocolate and coffee into the egg mixture.
7. Fold in the egg whites which have been beaten stiff.
8. Spread this filling between the layers.
9. Chill overnight in the refrigerator.
10. Beat the whip cream flavoured with vanilla.
11. Use this to decorate the top with rosettes.

12. Sprinkle with grated chocolate and thin slices of preserved ginger.

ALICE THOMSON

Chocolate Truffle Cake

Irene Say likes this dessert because you do not have to bake it.

Equipment
a nine inch springform cake pan
a 10 inch or larger round serving platter

Ingredients
6 oz of Amaretto biscuits
16 oz of semi-sweet chocolate
5 tablespoons of light corn syrup
5 tablespoons of rum or your favourite liqueur such as Amaretto
2 cups of heavy whipping cream
a selection of fresh fruit for garnishing

Method
1. Grease the cake pan with butter.
2. Crush biscuits with a rolling pin and press the biscuits into the bottom of the pan.
3. Melt the chocolate in a double boiler.
4. Stir in rum and corn syrup.
5. Beat cream until slightly thickened in a large bowl.
6. Fold half of the cream into the chocolate mixture, now removed from heat.
7. Fold that mixture into the rest of the cream.
8. Pour into the springform pan, cover with plastic wrap and chill overnight.
9. Run a flat knife around the sides to loosen.
10. Lift base of pan with cake onto a large round platter.
11. Use a sieve to dust the surface with cocoa powder.
12. Serve thin slices (it is very rich) with fresh fruit such as mandarin orange segments or strawberries and kiwis. Slices of star fruit

would be appropriate in the holiday season.

Irene Say

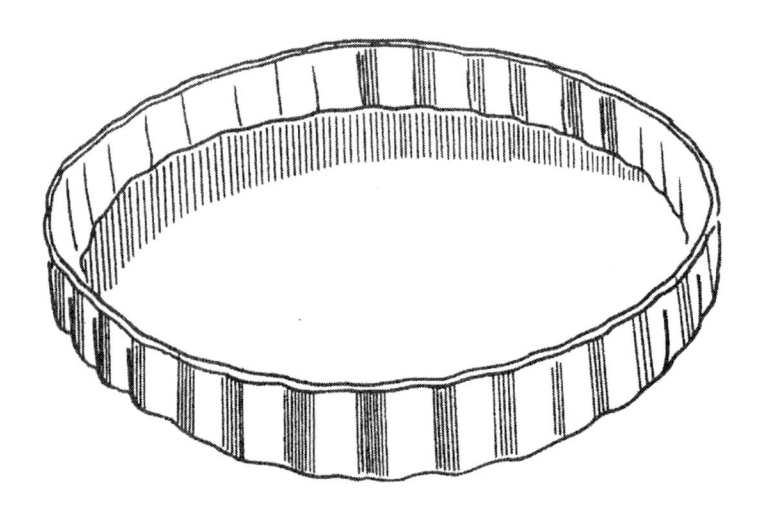

Fruit Tarts

Kate Rapson, Vice Chair of the Woodfield Association, and her husband, Jeff Carson, live in West Woodfield. Jeff's grandmother, Julia Krabacz, who was originally from Hungary, was known for her brandied peach butter and shared the recipe with Kate and Jeff. It is quoted in the original for those who want to make several jars of an authentic preserve.

Brandied Peach Butter

5 cups mashed peaches
4 cups sugar
1/4 cup brandy
Mash peaches.
Simmer until cooked about one half hour.
Add sugar and cook until thick - three-quarters of an hour.
Remove from stove.
Add brandy.
Put in jars and seal.

Kate Rapson
Kate has used this spread as an appetizer with crusty bread and cheese.

The following version from our test kitchen, has a few alterations which produces a smaller amount, just two cups of a tasty spread, which can be kept refrigerated and used up in a short time.

Ingredients
---
4 large peaches - free stone
1 cup of white granulated sugar which had been stored with a vanilla bean in the jar
1/4 cup of brandy

Method
1. Blanch the peaches in a pot of boiling water for a few minutes to make them easier to peel.
2. Cut the peeled peaches into small chunks.
3. Use a potato masher to make a purée of peach in a heavy saucepan.
4. Simmer uncovered for about one half hour until cooked.
5. Add one cup of sugar and bring to a rolling boil.
6. Control the heat for about three-quarters of an hour, until purée has thickened.
7. Remove from the stove and add the brandy.
8. A whizz with an immersion blender makes a smooth spread.

Although the amount of sugar was cut, the result seemed sweet enough but feel free to adjust. Note that the brandy was not reduced but it did not seem too strong.

This spread is the perfect base for a

Brandied Peach Tart

Equipment
a rectangular tin baking pan with a removable bottom (see supplier list)
or a round 9 inch fluted tin
parchment paper and raw beans for baking the pastry blind

Ingredients
pastry to line pan (see recipe to follow)
5 or 6 medium peaches, enough to cover the pan in overlapping slices
1 cup of peach spread
honey, sugar or jam for glazing

Method
1. Preheat oven to 425F.
2. Roll the chilled dough 1/8 of an inch thick to fit your pan. Place into buttered pan.
3. Line it with parchment paper and fill with dried beans to pre-bake or set the crust. This is a useful procedure to follow when baking

quiche, etc. as it prevents soggy crusts. The beans can be stored in a jar for repeated use.
4. Pre-bake pastry for about 5 minutes.
5. Turn oven down to 375F.
6. Remove pastry shell from oven. Lift out beans and reserve.
7. Spread brandied peach butter or jam over the base.
8. Blanch, peel and slice the peaches.
9. Layer slices in overlapping rows to completely cover the crust.
10. Sprinkle with a little sugar if fruit not sweet enough.
11. Bake in moderate oven for 30 to 35 minutes.
12. Brush on some melted honey or suitable jam for a light glaze.

ANN LINDSAY

MAKE THIS RECIPE YOUR OWN.

Line the crust with slices of pear. Dot the rows with prunes softened in sherry or honey.

Alternate rows of raspberries, blueberries and strawberries when in season.

Versatile Pie Pastry

Depending on the proportions of fat used, this pastry can be adjusted for traditional apple pie, French fruit tarts or rich flans. Some basic procedures remain the same for all pastry making:

    Have all ingredients very cold.
    Work quickly.
    Chill dough for a few hours prior to rolling.

Equipment
a food processor fitted with the steel blade or a metal pastry blender

Ingredients
for two 9 inch shells:
2 cups pastry flour
1/2 teaspoon salt or sugar (depending on the filling)
4 oz of shortening
2 oz of butter (reverse these amounts for a richer crust)
5 to 6 tablespoons of ice water

Method
1. Place flour either in the bowl of the processor or in a mixing bowl.
2. Add salt or sugar if a sweet crust is desired.
3. Cut shortening and/or butter into cubes. Drop into bowl.
4. Work quickly to cut fat into flour until granules are the size of navy beans. Or whirl machine with off/on rapid motions.
5. Dribble in ice water with machine running until pastry just forms a ball. Stop immediately.
6. Sprinkle a little flour on parchment or wax paper. Wrap the ball of dough and refrigerate.
7. Cut it in half to roll out on floured surface.

Variations

The richer butter and sugar pastries are preferred for open fruit tarts such as apricot, pear, plum.

Savory quiches and meat fillings are usually baked in a crust made with a higher percentage of shortening or without butter. As are the traditional covered apple pies.

Ann Lindsay

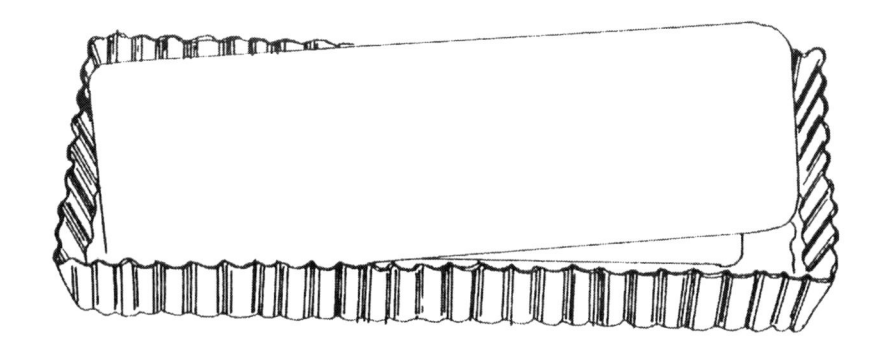

The Bishop's Snow Pudding

The name of our community, Woodfield, is taken from the name of the Cronyn family residence, (originally The Pines), a field stone mansion built on Dundas Street near Adelaide about 1839. It was the home of the Reverend Benjamin Cronyn who became the first Anglican Bishop of Huron and the grounds extended over beyond what is now Princess Avenue. The following recipe comes from a descendent, Dorey Jackson:

"I have a recipe for Lemon Snow Pudding that I received from my grandmother Dorothy Cronyn, (Richard Hume Cronyn) which was originally Bishop Benjamin Cronyn's."

Ingredients

1 tablespoon unflavoured gelatin
1/4 cup cold water
2/3 cup boiling water
4 thin lemon rinds
2 egg whites
4 tablespoons lemon juice
2/3 cup sugar

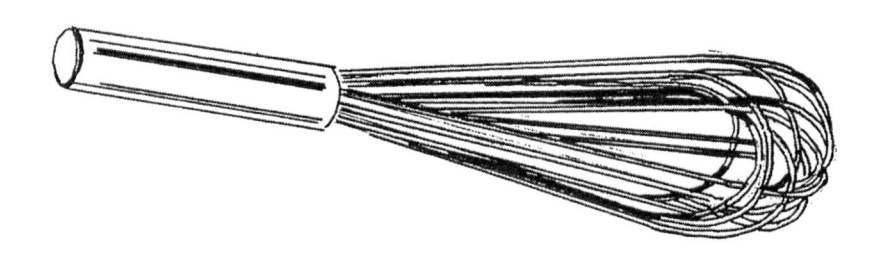

Method

1. Soften gelatin by sprinkling it over 1/4 cup cold water.
2. Combine rind, boiling water, and sugar in a saucepan and stir.
3. Bring to a boil, cooking for 5 minutes.
4. Remove rind and add gelatin and lemon juice.
5. Chill until syrupy, stirring occasionally to prevent a skin. (About 45 minutes to 1 hour.)
6. When partially set, beat until foamy.
7. Beat egg whites until stiff and combine. Continue beating until stiffening begins.
8. Wet serving bowl or sherbert glasses before pouring into it.
9. Top with grated lemon zest or fuit in a little juice after it has set.

Cheers,
Dorey Jackson, Daughter of Barbara Jackson (Cronyn)

Danish Fruit Pudding

This is a dessert which visitors to Denmark struggle to pronounce in Danish even before they have ever had a taste of it. It is called Rødgrød (Red Pudding), and when you add with cream it becomes Rødgrød med Fløede. The Danes take great delight in hearing it being mispronounced again and again!! There are many variations of this dessert throughout Scandinavia. This is the one that works for me and which I make once a year when the berries are available at the Market. However, it can of course be made with frozen berries, but it somehow loses its charm and authenticity.

Ingredients
12 oz red currants
12 oz raspberries
12 oz cherries
12 oz black currants
(Or any other berry combination)
Sugar to taste (approximately 4 oz for 10 cups of juice
10 tablespoons of corn starch

Method
1. Rinse the berries, strip the currants off the stems, take the stalks off the cherries and put all the fruit into a large saucepan and cover with cold water.
2. On top of the stove bring the juice to a boil at slow heat and boil for about 10 to 15 minutes.
3. Strain the juice twice, measure it (if necessary dilute with a little water to bring it to 10 cups and pour it back into the saucepan).
4. Add sugar to taste, approximately 4 oz for 10 cups of juice.
5. Dissolve the cornstarch in 1/2 cup of cold water and add to the juice while whisking vigorously, making sure it doesn't go lumpy.
6. Pour into individual dessert bowls or a couple of larger glass serv-

ing bowls.
7. Sprinkle a tiny bit of sugar on top and chill for at least 4 hours.
8. Before serving decorate with a few slivers of blanched almonds and pass a pitcher of cream (preferably whipping cream) separately.

ULLA TROUGHTON

Spirited Fruit Crisps

Hazel Elmslie has served on the Woodfield Community executive for a number of years. She keeps track of whether or not your membership fees are due. As an assistant financial planner, she has recipes neatly filed for decades. An old Gourmet recipe for pear crisp has inspired many other fruit desserts. Over time, Hazel has adapted it to suit what happens to be in her pantry.

Equipment
a 12″ by 14″ oval au gratin dish

Ingredients
For the classic crumble mix:
1-1/2 cups large flat rolled oats
1/4 cup flour
1 cup packed dark brown sugar
1 teaspoon cinnamon
1/2 teaspoon finely grated root ginger or ginger powder
a few scrapings from a whole nutmeg
1/4 teaspoon salt
2 tablespoons liqueur or spirits
1/2 cup unsalted butter

For the fruit
Crisps can be made with apples, plums, cherries, pears, or peaches. In the summer, you can mix an endless variety of fresh berries. Two pounds of fruit will fill the au gratin dish.
I confess to keeping the cupboard stocked with tins of pears and peaches, already peeled, cored, sliced and ready for the next step.
I've been inventive with the choice of spirits.
2 tablespoons of a pear brandy, such as Poire William if you are using pears.
2 tablespoons Calvados if apples are your choice.

Kirsch complements cherries.
Old Prune marries well with plums.
Frangelico is perfect with peaches.
In a pinch, I've used rum, rye or Stone's Ginger Wine.
1 tablespoon lemon juice
2 tablespoons fruit powdered sugar (fine granulated)

METHOD

1. Preheat oven to 350F.
2. Combine the oats, flour and spices in a large bowl.
3. Cream the brown sugar, butter and 2 tablespoons of liqueur. Have another 2 tablespoons handy for the assembly.
4. Use your fingers to make a crumbly mixture of the dry ingredients and the creamed ingredients.

ASSEMBLY

1. Peel, core and quarter, halve or slice the fruits if large.
2. In a small bowl mix the lemon juice, the 2 tablespoons of spirits and the sugar.
3. Toss the fruit in this mixture.
4. Butter the gratin dish thoroughly.
5. Arrange the fruit in overlapping rows in the dish.
6. Spread the oat mixture over to cover evenly.
7. Bake at 350F for 45 minutes.

HAZEL ELMSLIE

EDITOR'S NOTE

The spring after Hazel moved into her home, she uncovered a very fragrant antique quartered-rosette bush, which had been buried under an elm hedge for years. It now spills over the sidewalk and has been the source of many cuttings offered at the annual plant exchange. Because there is a rose type called Brandy, with a heavy, fruity scent, it might be appropriate to sprinkle a few drops of rosewater over your baked crumble for a truly unique Woodfield Rose Dessert.

Applesauce Cake Roll

We have made this recipe a few times over the years for some of our Woodfield neighbours.

Ingredients

3 eggs
3/4 cup sugar
8 oz. applesauce
1 cup sifted all purpose flour
1/2 teaspoon baking powder
1/2 teaspoon baking soda
1/2 teaspoon ground cinnamon
1/4 salt
1/4 teaspoon ground cloves
1 cup whipping cream
1/3 cup chopped walnuts

Method

1. Preheat oven to 350F.
2. In a small bowl beat eggs until thick, preferably with an electric mixer. Then add sugar beating well.
3. Add 1/2 cup applesauce.
4. Sift together flour, baking powder, baking soda, cinnamon, salt and cloves.
5. Fold into egg mixture.
6. Spread onto greased and floured 15″ by 10″ by 1″ jelly roll pan.
7. Bake at 350F for 15 to 20 minutes.
8. When the sponge is cooked, immediately loosen sides and invert onto towel sprinkled generously with powdered sugar.
9. Roll up carefully. Let cool on rack.
10. Whip cream until soft peaks form and fold in remaining applesauce and walnuts.

11. When cake is cool unroll carefully and spread applesauce mixture over cake.
12. Roll cake up again carefully on wax paper to cover and then cover with foil and chill. (If you get a crack just turn it so that it is hidden).
13. Garnish with additional whipped cream or dust with icing sugar.

Enjoy! We think it tastes better the second day.

P. STONE

Poppy Seed Cake

This recipe was given to us by Sue Wilson, who lived on Peter Street for many years and was an active member of the Woodfield Community.

Ingredients

1 cup milk
1/2 cup poppy seeds
1/2 cup butter
1-1/2 cup sugar
3 eggs
1 teaspoon vanilla
2 cups all purpose flour
3 teaspoons baking powder
1 teaspoon salt

Method

1. Preheat oven to 350F.
2. Combine milk and poppy seeds. Set aside.
3. Cream butter and sugar, beat until fluffy
4. Add 3 egg yolks and vanilla and beat until light.
5. Sift flour, baking powder and salt.
6. Add alternately with milk, poppy seed mixture beginning and ending with flour, blending after each addition.
7. Beat 3 eggs whites until stiff, but not dry. Fold into batter.
8. Pour into 9˝ by 12˝ by 2˝ glass cake pan, greased and sprinkled with flour.
9. Bake at 350 F for 45 minutes.
10. Frost with a butter icing.

Lemon Butter Icing

Ingredients
4 oz butter
8 oz icing sugar
1 teaspoon very fine grated lemon
2 teaspoons lemon juice

Method
1. Place the softened butter in a mixing bowl and sift the icing sugar over the top.
2. Add the grated lemon and the lemon juice and cream all the ingredients together with a wooden spoon until well blended.

P. Stone

My Grandmother's Cheesecake

My family was Danish and lived in Tavistock near Stratford where I was raised. My grandmother was a cheesemaker who worked for many years at the Tavistock Cheese Company, where she would have obtained the fresh cream cheese, sour cream and butter required for this recipe, created during this time. I got the recipe from my mother about twenty-five years ago. My grandmother lived with us when she was older and I remember that she spent all her time in our kitchen where she cooked many wonderful dishes.

Equipment

10 inch springform pan, lightly greased
1 good rubber spatula
1 measuring cup
Have everything out on counter first, so that ingredients are at room temperature.

Ingredients For the crust:

1-3/4 cups graham wafer crumbs
1/4 cup finely chopped walnuts
1/2 teaspoon cinnamon
1/2 cup butter

Ingredients For the filling:

2 8oz packages of cream cheese or preferably 1 lb of bulk cream cheese
1 cup sugar
3 eggs (at room temperature)
3 cups sour cream
2 teaspoons vanilla.

Method

1. Preheat oven to 350F.
2. In a 4 to 6 cup capacity bowl, rub butter into the rest of the ingredients for the crust until well mixed and pat into bottom of 10 inch springform pan.
3. In a 6 to 10 cup capacity bowl, mix all ingredients for the filling together in electric mixer, food processor or with electric hand mixer until almost liquid.
4. Use spatula and slowly pour onto crust.
5. Bake in the middle of preheated oven for 50 to 60 minutes. Take a peek at 50 minutes to see how it is.
6. When cool decorate with a variety of toppings: toasted sliced almonds, sliced kiwis, blueberries, raspberries, cherries in sauce, or a mixture in the middle of the cheesecake.

John Wegman

John has also made this cake using 3 cups of cream cheese and 2 cups of sour cream. This produces a thicker cheesecake.

Sour Cream Pudding

Janice Lemieux is a new Woodfield resident and is delighted with her move here. She is already becoming involved in neighbourhood activities. Janice is submitting a recipe handed down from her grandmother. The family were crop farmers in the Dutton area and most of the family recipes are for rather hearty dishes for hard working farmers. This is a quick and easy light pudding that would have been a fitting dessert to one of those hearty meals.

Ingredients

1 cup sour cream
1 egg
1/2 cup sugar
2/3 cup flour
1 teaspoon baking powder
1 teaspoon soda
1/8 teaspoon nutmeg
pinch of salt
1 apple sliced (optional)

Method

1. Preheat oven to 350F.
2. Beat egg with sugar until light and foamy.
3. Mix baking powder and soda, salt and nutmeg with flour.
4. Add flour mixture and sour cream to egg mixture to make batter.
5. Pour half the batter into a greased, 1 pint baking dish, cover with a layer of apple slices (if using) and pour the rest of the batter over.
6. Bake for 30 minutes or until firm.
7. Serve with brown sugar sauce.

Ingredients for Brown Sugar Sauce

1 cup brown sugar
1/4 cup butter
3/4 cup warm water
1-1/2 tablespoons corn starch
1/2 teaspoon pure rum flavouring.

Method

1. Melt butter, add brown sugar and cook over low heat for 10 minutes, stirring occasionally to prevent burning.
2. Add water and bring to boil and stir until mixture is dissolved.
3. Mix cornstarch with a little cold water and add to sauce. Cook until thickened.
4. Remove from heat and add flavouring.

Janice Lemieux

Make this pudding your own.

Add a few raisins to taste either in addition to or instead of apples. Flavour batter with lemon juice.

A Sweetheart Date Cake

Our archivist, Glen Curnoe, knocked on the door with another early cook book, this time from a company who provided London women with their spices, coffee, flavouring extracts, and baking needs. His grandmother lived in East London, where the IXL Spice Company plant was located in the first decade of the 1900's and she used their products faithfully. She probably also collected the coupons that came in each package to be redeemed for impressive quality crystal bowls, jardinieres, tea sets and even kitchen cabinets (829 coupons).

The products were packaged with the name Sweetheart Brand and a fetching Gibson Girl portrait beside the reassuring word, Pure. In 1928, IXL was bought by Gorman and Eckert. Mr. Richard C. Eckert lived in Woodfield at 434 Queens Avenue (now demolished). He attended Cronyn Memorial Church and the Mocha Temple. In 1959 Gorman and Eckert sold to Baltimore based McCormick and Company. The London operation, now on Clarke Road, still supplies condiments and baking needs to London households.

Here is a recipe from the circa 1910 Sweetheart Brand Cookbook.

Equipment

You need a baking pan that will hold 6 cups of batter half way. I used three 6˝ by 3-1/2˝ by 2-1/2˝ inch loaf tins, as I intended to present slices with a cheese and apple as a dessert. A 10 ˝ springform cake tin would produce a lovely rich cake worthy of a cream cheese icing.

Ingredients

1 cup brown sugar
4 oz. butter
2 eggs
1/2 cup warm water
1-1/2 cups flour

1 teaspoon baking soda
1 lb. chopped dates - soaked in a little warm water if dry
1 cup chopped walnuts
1 teaspoon vanilla

METHOD

1. Preheat oven to 350F.
2. Butter a 9˝ by 4˝ loaf pan or a round 10˝ cake tin.
3. Cream the sugar with the butter.
4. Beat in the eggs and warm water.
5. Sift the soda with the flour.
6. Combine the flour and sugar mixtures. Beat to form a smooth batter.
7. Fold in the dates, walnuts and vanilla.
8. Bake for one hour and fifteen minutes if you are using a large, round cake pan. It may need even longer. Check with a skewer inserted in the centre. I used three small loaf tins and they required one hour, 20 minutes.

SWEETHEART BRAND COOKBOOK

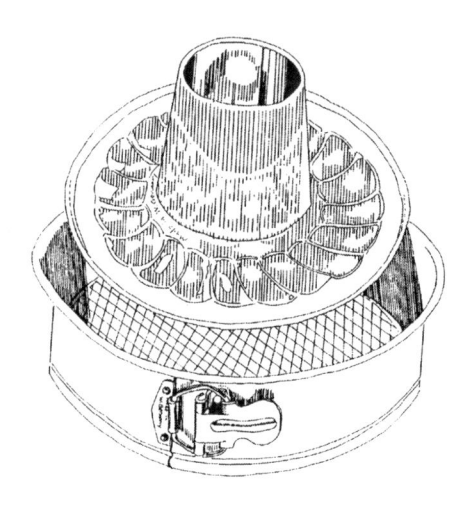

Ice Cream Memories

Many favourite desserts feature ice cream. Simple treatments can make lasting memories.

Ice Cream Affogato al Caffe

Michael and I always enjoyed eating ice cream (gelato) when in Italy. The following dessert was one of our favourites.

Ingredients
Per person:
A couple of scoops of vanilla ice cream in a dessert bowl
1/2 cup (demi tasse) of espresso coffee
1 shot of Frangelico (hazelnut liqueur)

Method
Bring all the ingredients to the table and let your guests do the work.

Vanilla Ice Cream with Hot Chocolate/Mint Sauce

The following recipe is my version of a favourite Danish dessert often called
Coupe Copenhagen.

Ingredients
vanilla ice cream
To make the hot chocolate/mint sauce:
5 oz of good quality semi-sweet chocolate chips
1 oz butter
1/2 cup water
1 tablespoon cream
1 tablespoon crème de menthe

METHOD
1. Melt the chocolate and the water in a small pan on top of the stove.
2. Add the butter, the cream and the crème de menthe.
3. Take a dessert bowl, or better still, a parfait glass for each person and fill with a couple of scoops of vanilla ice cream. Pour the hot chocolate/mint sauce over the ice cream and serve.

LEMON ICE CREAM

Danish friends, Birgit and Claus Santon, made this dessert for Michael and I once when we visited them in Nice, Provence. I believe it was something they dreamt up.

INGREDIENTS
1 liter of vanilla ice cream
juice of 2 lemons
1/2 cup of vodka

METHOD
1. Blend all the ingredients in the food processor until almost liquid
2. Serve in martini glasses
3. Decorate with an Italian wafer (cigarette style) and a straw.

Serves four

ICE CREAM WITH STREGA

Strega is an Italian liqueur which we were introduced to in Florence in the 1960's. Many years later we had it served over ice cream in an Italian restaurant in London (England), and when we returned to Canada we created the following recipe from memory.

INGREDIENTS
vanilla ice cream
almond macaroons
a few ounces of Strega

Method
Per person:
1. Put one almond macaroon sprinkled with Strega in the bottom of a parfait or martini glass.
2. On top of macaroon put one scoop of vanilla ice cream.
3. Add another macaroon followed by a second scoop of ice cream.
4. Pour Strega over top.
5. Decorate with almond macaroons or chocolate.

Ulla Troughton

Make this recipe your own.

You can try several other interesting combinations to make your own memories:

Pass a bottle of Irish Cream to pour over a dish of chocolate ice cream.

Grand Marnier is a treat on any citrus flavour frozen dessert.

How about a dribble of Scotch on a scoop of butterscotch ice cream?

Serve a small shortbread with the butterscotch ice cream.

Sit a brandied cherry on top.

Shave on some dark chocolate.

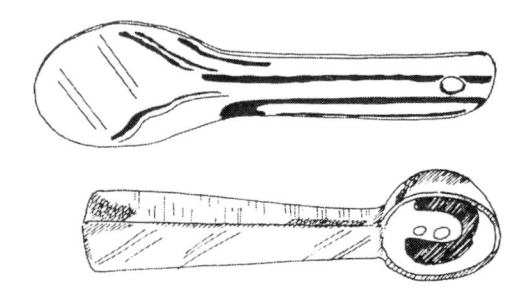

BREAD AND BAKED GOODS

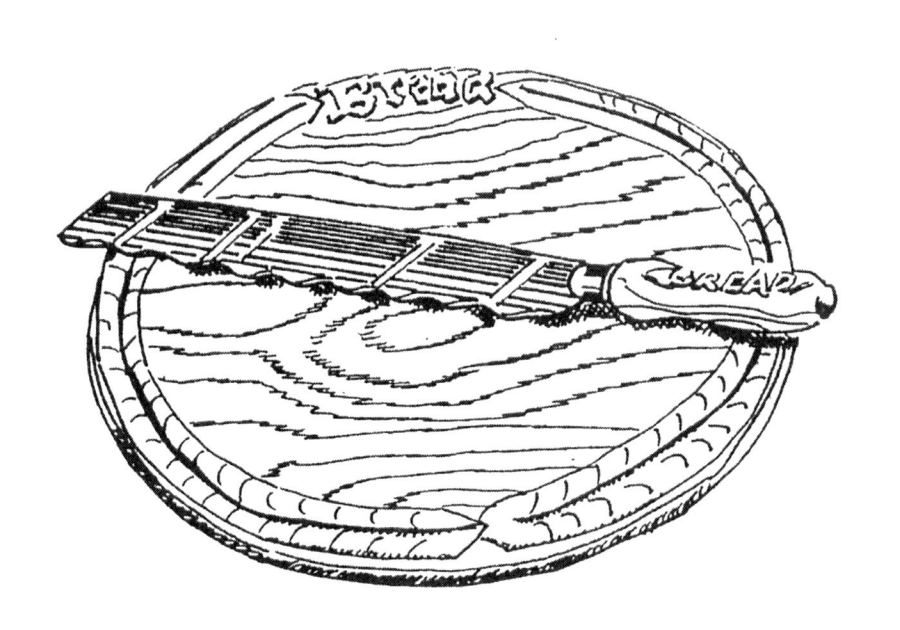

Hope Lodge Bagels

Several years ago, before we were married, my wife Jennifer underwent surgery for brain cancer. The surgery was successful but required a very specialised follow-up treatment for three months in Boston. We were very fortunate in being able to take advantage of The American Cancer Society's Hope Lodge programme, which provides free lodging for patients from out of town. We were located in a Hope Lodge in Worcester, Massachusetts. Every morning Jennifer and other residents were shuttled into Boston for treatment and every morning before they left my bagels became their staple breakfast. I developed the recipe for the bagels and was really delighted when the other patients, hospital staff and various Hope Lodge volunteers said they were better than New York bagels. Jennifer returns annually as a key speaker at their main fundraising event, accompanied by me and a bag of the bagels.

Ingredients

2-1/2 cups lukewarm water
6 cups flour
6 tablespoons brown sugar
1-1/2 teaspoons salt
6 teaspoons yeast
1 egg
2 tablespoons sugar
a choice of toppings - dried herbs, cheese, chopped onion, poppy or seseme seeds

Method

1. Preheat oven to 400 F.
2. Add brown sugar, salt and yeast to a large non-reactive bowl.
3. Add 2-1/2 cups lukewarm water to above ingredients.
4. Wait until yeast starts to bubble and then add 5 cups of flour.

5. Stir with a fork until your arm gets tired and then dump out on a lightly floured horizontal surface.
6. Knead in the final cup of flour...you may need less than cupful...or you may need some more. Keep going until the dough is elastic, not too sticky but will still bond to itself with some effort.
7. Cut the dough into 16 equal pieces; work them into smooth balls and cover with flour.
8. Cut 16 strips of paper about 2˝ by 8˝. Space the paper out on a horizontal surface. Make sure you don't need this real estate for at least 8 hours. Pinch a hole through the centre of the dough balls and stretch them out. Place one on each piece of paper. The paper is to help you pick them up later. Let the bagels rise (about 8 hours). Don't touch them, don't smell them and don't even think about them. If you do, you risk the fate of having them deflate.
9. When the bagels have risen, boil 3˝ of water with 2 tablespoons of sugar in the largest saucepan you have. Only handle the bagels when you absolutely have to. If you handle them too much THEY WILL DEFLATE. Gently pick up one of the bagels by the paper and place the bagel in the boiling water (discarding the paper). Boil the bagels for 1 minute and then gently flip it with a spatula. Boil for 1 minute on the reverse side. Place boiled bagels on a rack to cool.
10. Beat one egg. This egg is to be used as a wash, so that whatever topping (cheese, onion, poppy seeds etc...) you decide to put on your bagels, will stick. It will also give it a nice sheen after baking.
11. Brush the bagels with the beaten egg and apply the toppings if you use one (I like 5 year old Gouda).
12. Bake for about 15 minutes...you will know when they are done.
13. Look at that!! Wash your hands and eat. When they come out of the oven they don't even need butter.

Dana Berman

Old Fashioned Gingerbread

Glen Curnoe's cousin recently gave him a booklet entitled, "How to Use Your McClary Range", presented to her mother by the company when she purchased a new stove in 1940. She worked for this historic firm for several years.

John McClary and his brother Oliver opened a tinsmith shop in London Ontario, 1847. They peddled some of the earliest pots and pans to housewives door-to-door and were so well received that they opened a foundry for the manufacture of stoves and furnaces a few years later in the city core, on the site of what is now Citi Plaza. Their cast iron stoves boiled coffee in the cabooses of CPR trains as they puffed across Canada. As they grew more successful, the family assumed important roles in our community. John was a trustee of Wellington Street Church, vice-president of London Life, and eventually chairman of General Steel Wares of Canada. McClarys lived in Woodfield at 400 Queens Avenue, on the northeast corner of Colborne Street.

This gingerbread recipe has only five lines in the stove pamphlet. We have rewritten it with more detailed instructions so that you can bake it in your modern stove.

Equipment

A nine inch square non-stick baking pan is recommended. The McClary brothers originally sold tin ones to nineteenth century households in our neighbourhood.

Ingredients

3 tablespoons butter
1/2 cup sugar (we used brown)
1 beaten egg
1-1/2 cups flour
1/4 teaspoon salt

1-1/2 teaspoons ginger
1 teaspoon cinnamon
1 teaspoon baking soda
1/2 cup sour milk (can substitute plain yogurt)
1/2 cup molasses (treacle is a tasty alternative)

Method

1. Preheat oven to 350F.
2. Either by hand with a wooden spoon and a large bowl, or using an electric mixer, cream together the butter and sugar.
3. Whisk the egg separately then beat into the mixture.
4. Sift all of the dry ingredients together.
5. Incorporate the flour mixture into the creamed mixture alternately with the sour milk and molasses: A couple of spoonfuls of flour, a few tablespoons of milk, a bit more flour, some molasses, more flour, etc. beating well after each addition.
6. Spatula evenly into a buttered pan. If it seems too thick, beat in a few dribbles of extra milk.
7. Bake at 350F for 35 to 40 minutes.
8. Serve with freshly whipped cream.

Scottish Scones

I don't recall my grandmother making these scones but with the name of Gordon she could have. Her daughter, my mother, certainly made them. If you think of scones as something light – these aren't! They are made with oats and are hearty and filling. We had them with tea many a day at home.

Ingredients
2/3 cup butter, melted
1/3 cup milk
1 egg
1-3/4 cups large flake rolled oats
1-1/2 cup flour
1/4 cup sugar
1 tablespoon baking powder
1/2 teaspoon salt
1/2 cup raisins

Method
1. Preheat oven to 425F.
2. Combine oats, flour, sugar, baking powder and salt.
3. Add melted butter, milk and egg to above.
4. Mix well and stir in raisins.
5. Pat mixture out onto a lightly floured surface with a fork to form a 12" by 9" rectangle.
6. Cut the dough into 4" by 3" rectangles and cut each rectangle in half to form triangles.
7. Place on a greased cookie sheet and bake at 425F for about 12 minutes.

I really like these and tend to want a larger portion. As a friend said once,

"These taste like more", so I cut the first large rectangle of dough down the middle lengthwise, making two rather than three divisions.

KIM HARRISON

Light Christmas Cake

Kate Rapson lives in the heritage district of West Woodfield and is the vice-president of our association. Family memories have evoked a special recipe.

"My grandmother and grandfather, Rev. Major Alex Rapson, lived in London from the 1950's to 1965. Alex was the minister at Hyatt Avenue United Church during this time. Grace was always baking for the church. Alex Rapson used to encourage the kids to visit the manse, which was just next door, after the service, to have one of Grace's sweets. She was a wonderful baker. Some of our best recipes come from her collection."

Ingredients

1/2 lb. blanched almonds, whole
1 lb. candied fruit
1/2 lb. red glace cherries
1/2 lb. green glace cherries
1/2 lb. white raisins
1/2 lb. shredded coconut
1/2 lb. softened butter
1/2 lb. granulated sugar
5 eggs
2 cups all-purpose flour
1-1/2 teaspoon baking powder
1 cup drained crushed pineapple
5 tablespoons pineapple juice

Method

1. Preheat oven to 250 F.
2. Sift flour and baking powder together. Set aside.
3. Mix first 6 ingredients together in a large bowl.
4. Dredge fruit and nut mixture with 1/3 of the flour mixture.

5. Cream butter and sugar together till light and fluffy.
6. Add eggs one at a time, beating after each egg.
7. Add five tablespoons of pineapple juice. Stir well.
8. Add cup of crushed pineapple. Stir well to mix.
9. Add flour mixture and fruit. Stir to mix well.
10. Pour into buttered and parchment paper lined large size Christmas cake pan or into parchment paper lined and buttered loaf pans to three-quarters filled.
11. Bake large cake for 2-1/2 hours in preheated oven. Loaf size will take less time. Test smaller tins after an hour. Cool before wrapping. Store in fridge or a cool place. This cake does not have to be aged. It can be eaten the day after baking.

KATE RAPSON

Turtle Oat Squares

Helen Albert makes these treats for her son Jack and daughter Alex. Dad Rick sneaks the odd one probably. Here is how Helen describes this popular confection which had been passed along to her by a co-worker:

"This is a teeth grinding, sugary sweet compilation that bars all calorie counting. I find it best to freeze these bars right after everyone has had a taste. A frozen turtle oat square can still be consumed, however it takes a considerable time to actually chew through it."

Ingredients
2 cups all purpose flour
2 cups oats
1 cup brown sugar, packed
1 teaspoon baking soda
1 cup butter, melted

Method
1. Preheat oven to 350F.
2. Combine the first four ingredients in mixing bowl, add melted butter and mix well.
3. Reserve 1-1/4 cups of the mixture for the topping.
4. Press remainder into greased 13" by 9" pan.
5. Bake at 350 F for 12 to 15 minutes or until golden brown.

Filling Ingredients
1 cup butter
1 cup brown sugar, packed
1/2 cup corn syrup
1 can (about 1-1/2 cups) sweetened condensed milk
1 bag (about 1 cup) milk chocolate chips

Method

1. Prepare filling by heating butter, sugar, corn syrup and sweetened condensed milk in a heavy saucepan.
2. Over medium heat, stir mixture until it boils.
3. Boil 5 minutes stirring continually as it burns easily and quickly.
4. Sprinkle chocolate chips over oatmeal base.
5. Pour caramel filling evenly over crust.
6. Sprinkle reserved oatmeal mixture.
7. Bake for 20 to 25 minutes longer or until golden.
8. Cool completely, and then cut into squares. Nibble one, then hide them fast.

Helen Albert

Gentlemen's Chocolate Kisses

When Glen Curnoe brought us his mother's copy of *"Smallman & Ingram's Cook Book"*, he introduced two prominent Woodfielders into our collection. John B. Smallman built a grand home at 468 Colborne Street in 1902, which is now the location of the Mocha Shriners. His partner, Lemuel H. Ingram, in 1881 had built 499 Dufferin Avenue, that Victorian gem with the elegant wrap-around porch on the west corner of Peter Street. In 1877 these men founded a dry goods business on the south side of Dundas Street at Richmond. Their business grew to include many other departments which by 1908 were housed in a handsome five-storey red brick building on this main corner. Up until 1945, Londoners would say, "Meet me under the clock at Smallman & Ingram."

Glen's mother worked at this department store from 1926 to 1935 and bought the Cook Book just prior to her marriage for 47 cents. The Cook Book was no doubt compiled to promote their kitchenwares department. Photographs of 1930's refrigerators and waffle irons abound. These old collections throw an interesting light on the food buying and cooking habits of seventy-five years ago. The dessert chapter seems the most appetizing. This recipe for chocolate nut kisses requires the use of an electric beater (from Smallman & Ingram).

Chocolate Nut Kisses

Ingredients
5 egg whites (at room temperature)
1-1/4 cups powdered sugar
1 cup chopped walnut pieces
1/2 teaspoon of pure vanilla
1-1/2 cups grated chocolate
1/8 teaspoon cream of tarter (helps whites to stiffen)

Method

1. Set the oven at 300F.
2. Line a baking sheet with parchment paper.
3. Beat the egg whites, pinch of cream of tarter and sugar together until firm. Having the whites at room temperature before you start helps them to stiffen quicker.
4. Fold in nuts and vanilla.
5. Blend in the grated chocolate.
6. Drop teaspoonfuls of the batter on the baking parchment.
7. Bake in the slow oven for about 15 minutes.
8. Transfer the baking sheet to a moist tea towel to cool and facilitate removal.

These amounts will make 6 dozen kisses from two Woodfield gentlemen, Smallman and Ingram.

Corn Bread

Ruth Hoch received this recipe from a colleague at the health unit in 1979. It has been a family hit ever since. "My brother loves it with maple syrup as a dessert. It also makes a great accompaniment to a pot of chili."

Ingredients
1/2 cup yellow cornmeal
1 cup whole meal or all purpose flour (or a mix of half each)
1/2 cup sugar
2 teaspoons baking powder
1/2 teaspoon baking soda
1/2 teaspoon salt
1 cup yogurt
1/2 cup milk
1 egg
1 tablespoon vegetable oil (such as sunflower or corn)

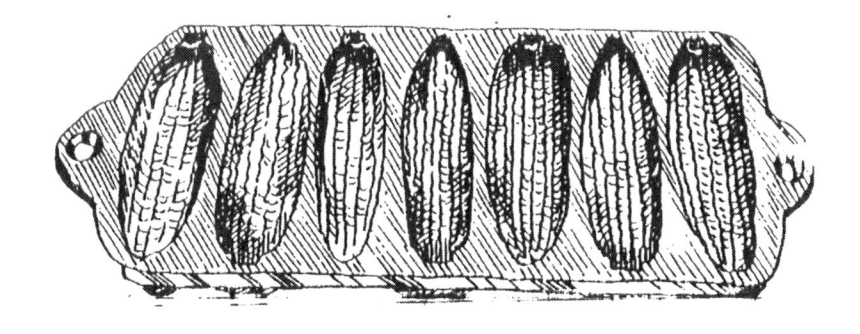

Method

1. Preheat oven to 425F.
2. Combine dry ingredients in a large bowl.
3. Whisk egg and oil in another bowl. Stir in yogurt and milk until smooth.
4. Make a well in the centre of dry ingredients.
5. Combine wet into dry just enough to blend.
6. Pour into greased 9˝ by 9˝ pan.
7. Bake at 425F for 20 minutes. Watch the timing closely at this high a heat.

Ruth Hoch

Make this recipe your own:

jalepeno peppers, seeded and chopped could be stirred into batter
grated cheddar or jack cheese
apple cubes

Lemon Bread

This recipe is a Bishop Cronyn fixture for receptions and another recipe from "Father's Favourites", a cookbook published by the Anglican Church Women in the 1950s.

Ingredients

6 tablespoons butter
1 cup granulated sugar
2 eggs, beaten
1-1/2 cups sifted flour
1 teaspoon baking powder
1/2 teaspoon salt
1/2 cup milk
grated rind and juice of 1 lemon

Method

1. Preheat oven to 325 F.
2. Cream butter and sugar together until light.
3. Add beaten eggs and mix well.
4. Add all other ingredients, mixing thoroughly.
5. Turn mixture into greased 8-1/2″ by 4-1/2″ by 2-1/2″ loaf tin and bake in middle of the oven for 1 to 1-1/4 hours.

Syrup

Make a syrup by mixing the juice of 1 lemon with 1/4 to 1/2 cup sugar. When the lemon bread is cooked and while it is still warm, pour the syrup over the loaf, adding a little at a time. Put back in oven for a few minutes only, to take away any stickiness

Anglican Church Women, Bishop Cronyn Memorial Church.

Freeport Egg Tarts

Bonnie MacLachlan's family roots are in the fishing village of Freeport, on Long Island, in the Bay of Fundy. In the nineteenth century, because trade was mostly local, citrus fruit was a rarity in this region. This old recipe – an approximation of lemon tarts – uses cider vinegar in place of lemon juice. Cider was plentiful because of the apple harvest in the Annapolis Valley.

INGREDIENTS

For the pastry:
1 cup regular flour, unbleached
1/3 cup shortening
pinch of salt
ice water to get the right texture

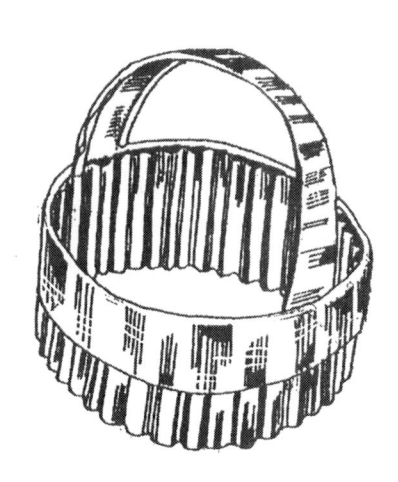

FOR THE CUSTARD:

2 eggs, beaten

1 cup sugar

5 tablespoons cider vinegar

1 teaspoon vanilla

pinch salt

METHOD

1. Preheat oven to 400F.
2. Make the pastry, roll it out, and line tart tins with it. (See page 210 for method.)
3. Mix the ingredients for the custard, and fill the tart shells.
4. Bake at 400° for 12 to 15 minutes.

Makes 18 small tarts, or 12 large ones.

BONNIE MACLACHLAN

Butter Tarts

There are two sides in the butter tart discussion. Those that favour corn syrup and raisins and those that favour currants and brown sugar. Well I was given the recipe for the latter nearly fifty years ago and I must say they are my favourite. Sinfully rich. I make them in tart tins which I can only find at Jill's Table on King Street. These are a lot shallower than muffin tins and easier for lining with pastry.

Ingredients

1/2 cup soft butter
3/4 cup sifted brown sugar
2 tablespoons milk or cream
1/2 cup currants
1 egg beaten
1 teaspoon vanilla
pastry for lining tart tins (see page 175)

Method

1. Preheat oven to 375F.
2. Cut circles of pastry to fit tart tins and place in tin.
3. Mix ingredients together and drop a teaspoon or so in patty tins.
4. Bake for 10 minutes until pastry is just coloured.

Makes 12 to 15 small tarts.

Hazel Desbarats

Prince Albert Cake

John E. Boomer founded Boomers Limited, a confectionery firm in London in 1881. Their Dundas Street premise was a favourite destination for lunch or afternoon tea. Walls decorated in wide vertical stripes of soft gray and strawberry pink, ornamental plaster work and oil paintings on canvas, set the scene for ice-cream and pastry rendezvous.

John's son, Herbert E. Boomer lived at 512 Colborne Street with his wife, Alice E. Boomer. Many recipes appear under her name in the May 1929 Selected Recipes Collection of the Women's Association of Metropolitan United Church.. This is one of them. We have clarified the instructions.

Equipment
The housewives of the twenties generally creamed and beat baked goods by hand. This recipe adapts very well to a food processor.

Ingredients
1/2 cup butter (a four oz stick)
1 cup brown sugar
2 beaten eggs
1-1/2 cups flour
3/4 teaspoon soda
1/2 teaspoon nutmeg
1 teaspoon cinnamon
1/2 cup sour cream or yogurt
1 cup chopped raisins

Method
1. Preheat oven to 350F.
2. Butter a 9 inch square pan or two smaller loaf pans.
3. Chop the raisins with a series of quick on/off pulses in the processor before you use it for the other ingredients. Or chop with a

chef's knife on a wooden board. Reserve them in a large mixing bowl.
4. Cream the butter and brown sugar until uniform in texture.
5. Whirl in the eggs.
6. Sift the spices and soda with the flour.
7. Add the dry ingredients alternately with the sour cream, beating each addition in well.
8. When all ingredients have formed a smooth, creamy batter, fold together by hand with the chopped raisins reserved in a bowl.
9. Spatula the mixture into a 9 inch buttered square baking pan or two 8˝ by 4˝ loaf pans.
10. Bake at 350F for about 35 minutes.

ALICE E. BOOMER

Generations of Shortbread

The frequent response to our plea for original recipes was, "But Ann, all recipes are based on earlier ones." True enough. To be more specific, we were hoping for recipes that had undergone a process, oral or written, that had reshaped them into family tradition. Here is an example of how that can happen. We start with a basic recipe from one of Bonnie Whitaker's relatives by marriage.

Shortbread Cookies

This recipe comes from Gladys Jones Newton an aunt of my first husband David. Gladys was born at 9 Prospect Avenue in 1894. I now live in that house. Her father Tom Jones built the three cottages on Prospect. The Jones family lived at 9 Prospect from 1887 to 1916. These cookies are a tradition in our family at Christmas and are referred to as Gladys' cookies.

The cookie was shaped in an unusual way and I will try and describe her method. Take a teaspoon of dough and flatten it on the cookie sheet with the heel of your hand. Take your middle finger and thumb and pinch the dough at 12 o'clock and 6 o'clock and 9 o'clock and 3 o'clock. Does that make sense??

Ingredients
1/2 pound butter (1 cup)
3/4 cup brown sugar, tightly packed
2-1/4 cups pastry flour

Method
Cream butter and brown sugar, stir in flour. Bake 10 to 12 min at 300F.

Bonnie Whitaker

That is the original e.mail of the recipe, received from Bonnie in May. At Christmas, our niece passed around a tray of shortbreads which her mother had taught her to bake, based on her grandmother Rheta's recipe. They tasted different from the recipe I had made from my Scottish grandfather for the past fifty years. Better in fact. Mine calls for rice flour and fruit powdered sugar. I asked our niece what her grandmother had used. "Cornstarch and icing sugar. And she sifted the dry ingredients three times!"

These are just three versions of countless ways of making shortbread, each cherished in family memories.

On New Year's morning, I decided to make a shortbread that would connect Gladys with Rheta.

This is how it goes.

Ingredients

1/2 lb butter (at room temperature)
3/4 cup brown sugar (tightly packed)
2 cups organic unbleached pastry flour
1/4 cup cornstarch

Method

1. Preheat oven to 300F.
2. Sift the flour and cornstarch three times and set aside.
3. Soften the butter with a stout wooden spoon or whirl it in a food processor.
4. Cream in the brown sugar until it is completely amalgamated, by hand or machine.
5. Add the sifted ingredients in several batches, mixing well after each.
6. Line a baking tray with parchment paper.
7. Using only a teaspoon of dough, flatten and shape each cookie as Bonnie describes.
8. These little coins should bake in between ten and fifteen minutes, depending on thickness.

Gladys, Bonnie, Rheta and Ann

MAKE THIS RECIPE YOUR OWN.

Gladys put a spot of jam in the centre of her cookies. You could try:
a walnut, pecan or almond
a piece of crystallized ginger
a chunk of white chocolate

Turn to page 301 to see how Wes Kinghorn customizes his shortbreads.

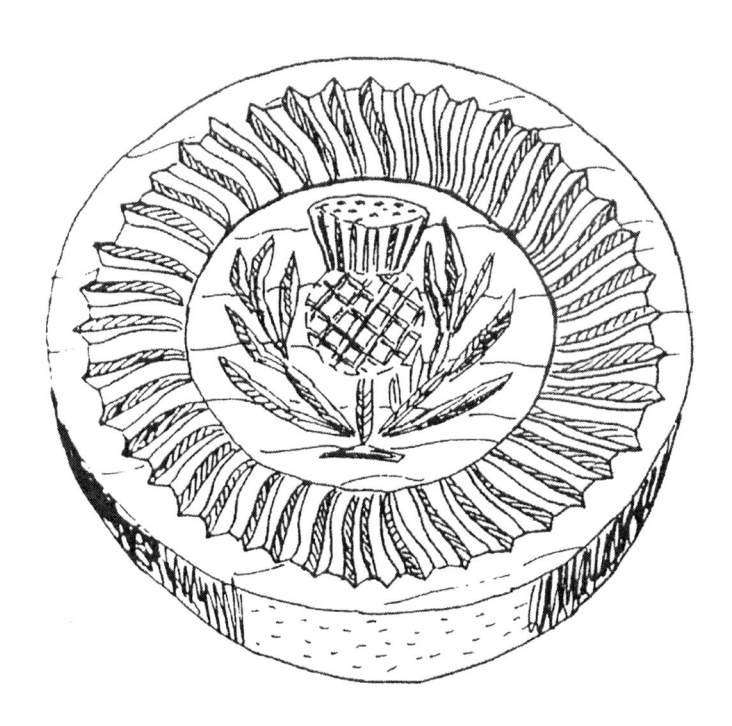

SEASONAL CELEBRATIONS

Spring Comes to Woodfield

It is tentative at first. Just the lightest tinge of green appearing on the trees. Dogs walking without their plaid coats. More cyclists and joggers whizzing past. Borders of daffodils and forsythia signal the actual arrival and get us hauling the spades out of the shed.

The City of London operates over twenty community garden sites. For a nominal fee residents can grow their own vegetables and herbs from May through October. Carling Heights is the garden site closest to Woodfield and many of us start planting lettuces, spinach, radishes, beets and leeks early in the spring. For quite a few years, Lord Roberts School set up a Maypole on the lawn and held gardening workshops the first week in May. Woodfield Community takes over their back playground area later in the month for our popular Plant Sale. Refreshments are offered as well as bags of compost.

Cranberry Yogurt Muffins

In time for the first frost free planting date, you will see garden enthusiasts wheeling barrow loads of iris roots, phlox clumps, trees and bushes toward the school grounds. They receive credit tickets for their transplant offerings, with which they buy other species they do not have. Margaret Howe, a seasoned Woodfield resident, who together with her late husband John, were the first clinical psychologists in private practice in London, opened their office in Woodfield in 1968. They immediately became involved in the community and Margaret has often brought these muffins of various kinds to events at Lord Roberts School and to the Plant Sale refreshment booth.

Ingredients

1 cup rolled oats

1 cup yogurt

1/2 cup vegetable oil

1 cup brown sugar

1 egg

1 cup all purpose flour

1/2 teaspoon salt

1/2 teaspoon baking powder

1 cup cranberries, chopped in half (blueberries or raisins may be substituted)

Method

1. Preheat oven to 400F.
2. Soak oats in yogurt.
3. Add oil, sugar and egg and beat well.
4. Sift in dry ingredients.
5. Before stirring, sprinkle berries over flour mixture and stir to blend.
6. Fill muffin cups and bake for approximately 20 minutes in 400F oven.

Makes 12 large or 24 small muffins

Margaret Howe

Carrot Cake Muffins

2009 was the first year I helped with the coffee and goodies station at the Plant Sale. These muffins I brought to sell at the bake goods booth were a last minute panic decision. I didn't have a good muffin recipe and I was wondering what I could make that would be worthy. This is originally a carrot cake recipe that I often get requests for and I thought I could make it as several batches of muffins instead. Neighbours enjoyed one with a coffee while they were plant browsing and I even sold half a dozen of them as a take-out order.

I altered the original standard version quite a bit by increasing the crushed pineapple and reducing the oil. I also halved the amount of sugar. For the icing I usually use a full package of cream cheese (eight ounces) instead of the three ounces suggested. (If you can barely taste it - why bother!)

Ingredients

2 cups shredded carrots
1 cup shredded coconut
1 cup chopped walnuts
19 ounce can of crushed pineapple, undrained
1/2 cup vegetable oil
1/2 cup raisins
3 eggs beaten
1 cup sugar
2 teaspoons vanilla
2 cups whole wheat flour
2 teaspoons baking soda
4 teaspoons cinnamon
1 teaspoon salt

Icing Ingredients

8 ounces cream cheese softened
1-1/2 tablespoons skim milk
2 tablespoons butter, softened
2 cups powdered sugar

Method

1. Preheat oven to 350F.
2. Combine carrots, coconut, walnuts, pineapple, oil and raisins. Set aside.
3. In a second bowl, whisk sugar into the beaten eggs. Stir in the vanilla and incorporate with the first mixture.
4. In a third bowl, mix flour, baking soda, salt and cinnamon. Fold it into the above mixture.
5. Line muffin tins with paper muffin cups and fill.
6. Bake at 350F for 25 to 30 minutes.

Icing

1. Cream all ingredients together.
2. Spoon into a piping bag fitted with a large fluted tip.
3. Pipe the icing into one large bud or a ring of small buds around each muffin.

Jennifer Prgesa

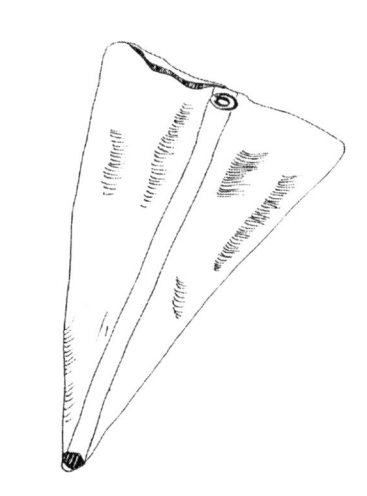

Salad of Herbs and Edible Flowers

Our home, in the residential core of the city, is girded with a ring of herbs and flowers. The garden sprang from inspirational seeds planted by gifted gardeners: a great aunt who grew tansy by a stream in Scotland; retired Londoners who created an herb garden walled by cedars so that they could work accompanied by bird song; the 17th century botanical garden of the herbalist Culpepper in England. Each spring our garden offers ingredients for a special salad composed of green leafy herbs and edible flowers.

Many of the following can be found in season in nurseries and markets. Make a selection according to your preferences and availability.

Greens	Herbs
baby spinach leaves	large leaf basil
endive	lovage - helps digestion
frisée	mints - purify
red oak leaf	fennel - for strength
arugula	chives
watercress	lemon balm - calming
leaves of Boston bib lettuce	chervil - protection from the plague

Arrange in a large white china or glass salad bowl. Toss gently with a dressing composed of:

1/3 good quality raspberry vinegar to 2/3 light olive oil. Sprinkle the flower petals around the edge of the bowl after tossing.

Flowers

Take care. Not all flowers are safe to eat. Some are poisonous. Consult a reliable guide for a list of edible plants. Here is a start for you. Make sure they have not been sprayed. Select four types maximum for best effect.

rose petals	violets	calendula petals
forget-me-nots	scented geranium	marigold petals
pansies	lavender	bergamot flowers
nasturtiums	pineapple sage	coriander blossoms
chive blossoms	blue borage	Johnny-jump-ups

Invite Titania and her company to gather round. Serve a punch bowl of May wine - a white Riesling infused with sweet woodruff blossoms.

THE GARDEN FAIRIES

Summerfests

Finally it's here! Roses, peonies and daisies replace the bulbs. Wicker furniture re-appears on the verandas. Neighbours call invitations across the street to each other to share a pot of tea or a bottle of rosé. Student parties break the stillness of long summer evenings.

The Pig Roasts in the school yard are now a legendary summer gathering. Rob Barney and Michael Troughton hefted a whole pig onto a spit and turned it over a trough of coals while the assembled community salivated over salad plates. We lined up for Rob to slice off a piece of succulent herb and garlic studded pork surrounded by crackling skin. Later, the ladies engaged in toss-the-slipper and cheesecake contests.

Now backyard barbecues are fired up to roast beer can chickens. Four submissions received testify to the popularity of this cooking method. We thought our neighbour's dinner was on fire, but it was just his "chook" (Aussie for chicken), spurting away. Here is Ashleigh Barney's recipe for definitive Roast Chicken. Perhaps we could revive Summerfest with rows of organic chickens roasting on spits.

Roast Chicken with Mustard Vinaigrette

This is a wonderful entrée for summer or winter. It can be roasted in the oven or the barbecue. Serve it hot, or prepare it a day ahead and serve cold for a dinner on the deck or at a picnic.

Ingredients
1 6 to 7 lb lovely fresh roasting chicken
1 large shallot, quartered
2 fresh rosemary sprigs
2 fresh sage sprigs
1 lemon sliced

1 cup mustard vinaigrette (See below)
1 tablespoon chopped fresh rosemary
1 tablespooon chopped fresh sage

Save additional rosemary and sage for garnish

Mustard Vinaigrette

1/4 cup Dijon mustard
3 tablespoons white wine vinegar
3/4 cup olive oil (not virgin)
2/3 cup chopped shallots
2 tablespoons chopped fresh rosemary
2 teaspoons chopped fresh sage

1. Mix mustard and vinegar in bowl.
2. Gradually whisk in oil. Add shallots and herbs.
3. Season with salt and pepper to taste. Can be made one day ahead. Bring to room temperature to use.

Makes approx. 1-1/2 cups.

Method

1. Preheat oven to 450F.
2. Wash chicken and pat dry. Salt cavity.
3. Place shallot, 2 each rosemary and sage springs and lemon slices in cavity.
4. Slide hand between chicken skin and meat over the breast to form pockets. Spread 2 tablespoons of the vinaigrette under the skin.
5. Tie the legs together and tuck wings under the body.
6. Season the chicken with salt and pepper. Rub vinaigrette over the body.
7. Roast at 450F for 20 minutes then reduce to 375F and roast for about 1 hour and 20 minutes. Check to see that juices run clear.

A great side dish to this is baby red potato salad with the above mentioned vinaigrette, boiled fresh green beans sprinkled with 1/3 cup of toasted walnuts chopped and any variety of crumbled blue cheese.

Add fresh berries and madeleines or gateau Breton for a perfect summer meal.

ASHLEIGH BARNEY

Rob Barney's Margarita

Rob and Ashleigh Barney lived in Woodfield during many of its formative years. Friends and neighbours were invited to their garden to greet the summer season with a glass or two from Rob's botttomless jug of Margaritas. His formula is handy for a party crowd as you do not have to make each one separately.

Equipment
a blender and proper wide-rim margarita glasses

Ingredients
lemon juice and coarse salt for frosting
2/3 can of frozen limeade (defrosted)
1 lime
2/3 of the limeade can of tequila
1/3 of the limeade can of Triple Sec
ice cubes

Method
1. Wipe the rim of the glasses with lemon juice and dip in salt to frost.
2. Fill a blender half full with ice cubes.
3. Add the limeade, tequila and Triple Sec.
4. Blend for about 30 seconds.
5. Pour into glasses and garnish with a wedge of lime.

Serves 4.

Rob Barney

For romantic purists, we offer the method for one glass.

The Classic Margarita

Equipment
a cocktail shaker and strainer

Ingredients
a slice of lime
kosher salt
freshly squeezed lime juice (1 tablespoon)
1-1/2 oz tequila
1/2 oz Triple Sec
3 or 4 ice cubes

Method
1. Rub the rim of a pre-chilled glass with the slice of lime and dip into the salt.
2. Shake the juice, tequila, Triple Sec and ice cubes in a tall glass or cocktail shaker which has a strainer over the top.
3. Place the strainer over the glass and pour the margarita through.

Serves 1

Secret Gardens

Last summer our community volunteered to help raise funds for The Children's Festival by opening their "Secret Gardens" to a tour. The day before, our president Wes was rebuilding his front steps to make an outdoor home for William the Mouse, who usually lives under his indoor staircase. Across the street, Joey McDowell had fairies swinging from tree branches and supping from bluebells. Linda Whitney has a truly secret garden hidden down a narrow path between her house and her neighbour. The design, sun exposure and colour tones of the plantings, all combine to give the sense of entering a Mediterranean garden. Linda and Mickey live that lifestyle in this beautiful space, enjoying impromptu meals with their neighbours, Hilary and Burton Moon and Jim and Judy Fentin.

Salad Caprese in il Giardino Secreto

Since this group of neighbours all vegetable garden together, meals tend to be produce they have just picked. One of their favourites is this classic combination.

Ingredients

6 ripe tomatoes
3 large mozzarella balls
12 large leaves of fresh basil
3 tablespoons of extra virgin olive oil (see supplier list for one infused with basil)
1 teaspoon red Balsamic vinegar
salt

Method

1. Cut the tomatoes using a serrated knife, into 1/4 inch slices.
2. Sprinkle lightly with salt.
3. Slice the mozzarella balls into the same thickness.
4. Alternate the slices of tomato and cheese across the salad plate.
5. Stack the basil leaves so that you can cut them into strips to scatter across the salad.
6. Stand back and admire the Italian colours on the plate - red, white, and green.
7. Dribble on the oil and vinegar.

Linda Whitney

Make this recipe your own

Sometimes this group of friends create towers by stacking alternate slices of the three main ingredients. If you have grown heritage tomatoes, you could compose a plate of many different coloured tomato slices.

Figs with Prosciutto

Mickey Apthorp adapts almost all their summer meals to include an inventive use of the barbecue. This appetizer course sounds downright decadent.

Ingredients

6 ripe figs (a neighbour one street over has a fig tree in a large pot in her garden)
6 slices of gorganzola or other rich blue cheese
6 slices of prosciutto
honey

Method

1. Cut the figs in halves or quarters length ways.
2. Sandwich them together with the ripe cheese.
3. Wrap each fig in a slice of prosciutto.
4. Put them on the grill for a few minutes until the cheese melts slightly.
5. Serve two halves on a plate dribbled with honey.

Mickey Apthorp

The Woodfield Café

Lawn Sale signs appear on telephone posts in June, urging buyers to come out to our annual sale of vintage goods from vintage homes. Now in its fourth year, we have many London dealers parking on our streets as early as seven a.m. to get the real finds. To the participants, this is another great chance to socialize. Alexandra and Michael Harkins transform their front lawn into a sidewalk café, setting up round bistro tables and collapsible chairs. A coffee urn and contributed baked goods provide the ambiance for exchange of tips on the bargains spread out on the neighbour's lawns. Proceeds from the café are donated to the "Trees for Woodfield" fund.

Harvestfest

When every lawn has rows of thirty leaf bags each neatly stacked for pick-up, we know that Harvestfest is around the corner. The third Thursday in November, Woodfield rents Dufferin Hall in the Masonic Temple and sets up long tables to hold about one hundred casseroles, salads, grains, meats, pastas and desserts. Each year the offerings seem to get better and the attendance larger. Donation tables display auction items from local businesses and the bidding is lively. The idea for producing this collection of recipes came from seeing and tasting the bountiful spread brought by our members. Here are a few samples from the past year's buffet tables.

Teriyaki Sweet and Sour Chicken Wings

Benedict and Helen Lockwood brought a platter of these tasty wings to their first Harvestfest after joining the neighbourhood. A good way to insure folks get to know you.

Ingredients
24 chicken wings
1/2 cup sweet and sour chili sauce
1/2 cup teriyaki soy sauce
2 tablespoon brown sugar
2 teaspoons lemon juice
2 tablespoons sesame seeds .

Method
1. Preheat oven to 425F.
2. Mix marinade ingredients together.
3. Toss the wings in a large bowl with the marinade and sesame

seeds.
4. Bake in a roasting pan at 425F for 45 minutes.

The Lockwoods suggest you make sure napkins are set out beside a platter of these delicious but gooey wings.

BENEDICT AND HELEN LOCKWOOD

Goodie's Roasted Vegetables

My friend Goodie shared this delicious recipe about 15 years ago. We enjoy it often during the fall and winter and try to use some vegetables from the community garden that Peter and neighbour Bonnie Whitaker grow together. This dish is always a crowd pleaser and cleanup is fast. Leftovers can be whirled with stock for a tasty, quick and nourishing soup.

Ingredients

1 medium eggplant cut in half length ways, then sliced into 1/2 inch rounds
4 small to medium zucchini – 2 yellow and 2 green cut in rounds or strips
4 cooking onions, peeled and cut into quarters
2 red or white waxy potatoes and 2 carrots, scrubbed and cut in chunks
2 peppers, 1 red and 1 yellow, seeded and cut into chunks
1 garlic bud, peel the cloves (cut small if cloves are large)
oregano, thyme and rosemary sprigs, fresh or dried herbs from the garden or from Covent Garden Market
1/4 cup olive oil
6 to 8 large plum tomatoes chopped into quarters for the top
salt and pepper to taste

Method

1. Preheat oven to 425 F.
2. Oil the bottom of a large roasting pan.
3. Steam or microwave all the potatoes and carrots together to soften (about 5 or 6 minutes).
4. Mix the veggies together in a big bowl with a little olive oil, the garlic sliced, and some of the herbs chopped.
5. Transfer veggies to the roasting pan.

6. Toss the rest of the herbs in a bit more oil and tuck them around the veggies.
7. Scatter the chopped plum tomatoes on the top.
8. Cover and bake for 20 minutes
9. Stir and remove the cover and bake for another 20 minutes until tender.
10. Salt and pepper to taste.

Variations for a one-dish meal

When the vegetables are nearly cooked, remove from the oven and tuck 8 portions of wild caught salmon (skin removed) into the vegetables. Cover and cook for 10 more minutes.

Serve in large soup or pasta bowls with a sprig of fresh rosemary and a slice of lemon.

Serves 8

Angie Killoran

Pear Tart

My Danish friend Marianne Stolt gave me this recipe many moons ago and I have made it every year when the pears are in season.

Ingredients
8 ounces flour
4-1/2 ounces butter
4 ounces sugar
1 teaspoon vanilla
1/2 teaspoon ginger
1 egg
about 6 ripe pears, peeled, cored and quartered
1 small carton of whipping cream

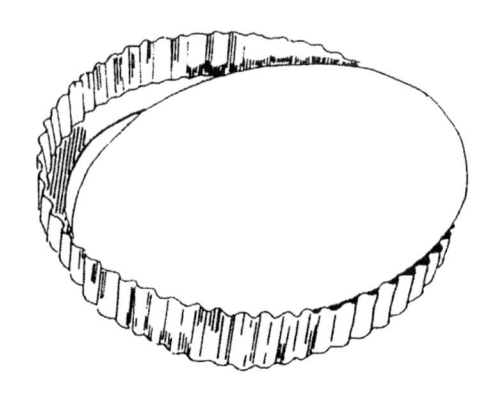

METHOD

1. Preheat oven to 400F.
2. Crumble the butter into the flour.
3. Add sugar, vanilla and ginger and mix with the egg.
4. Leave the dough in the fridge for about an hour.
5. Cut in half and roll it out to fit into a greased 10 inch tart pan with a fluted edge and a loose bottom.
6. Put the pears on top, rounded side up and side by side, use more pears if necessary.
7. Roll out the other half of the dough and put it on top of tart. Press the sides of the 2 layers of dough together and brush the tart with water.
8. Bake at 400 F for 40 minutes or until golden brown on top.

Serve with whipped cream.

ULLA TROUGHTON

Winter in Woodfield

On a rainy, chill November night, neighbours walk under the tall bare tree branches to a friend's house for dinner. They leave umbrellas on the porch and enter to be greeted by a wood fire and a candlelit table. They sit down to one of the hearty, nourishing soups in this collection.

Squash Soup

Living in an old double brick home can sometimes be chilly and a good bowl of soup can cure all! Near the end of fall, after I have been raking the inordinate number of leaves that somehow manage to fall on my postage stamp size front lawn, I like to warm up with a homemade soup like this.

Equipment

Immersion blender or upright blender
Cooking pot with cover (choose one with tall sides if using immersion blender to blend soup)

Ingredients

2 tablespoons grapeseed oil
4 cups cubed local buttercup or other winter squash
2 leeks (between 1 and 2 inches thick), chopped
3 to 4 cloves garlic
1/4 cup chopped fresh cilantro or 1-1/2 tablespoons dried cilantro leaves
2 cups water
2 cups organic chicken stock
1-1/2 teaspoons ground cumin
1/4 teaspoons freshly ground black pepper

Method

1. Heat grapeseed oil and then add squash, leeks, garlic and cilantro and sauté for about 10 minutes.
2. Add water and chicken stock and then cover the mixture to cook until the squash is soft.
3. Mix in cumin and black pepper.
4. Use immersion blender directly in the pot to blend the ingredients until desired smoothness or pour the ingredients into an upright blender and blend with the lid slightly open to avoid pressure build-up from the hot ingredients.

If you prefer a creamy soup, whirl in one half cup of 10% cream.

Jennifer Prgesa

An Evening of Carolling

Our traditional carol singing from door-to-door originated over twenty years ago at the Wolfe Street home of Ben and Briony Sterk. A group of brave hearts, bundled in woolens, led by Ben in his black cape and Spanish hat, could be seen wandering down snow-covered streets carrying red candles.

After they returned to Australia, the torch was picked up by the Troughtons who hosted the pre-carol festivities from their Prospect Avenue home. As we tuned our voices around the piano, Michael served hot spiced cider or a traditional Swedish punch.

Glögg

Traditionally the Swedish hot punch Glögg is made with Aquavit. This recipe is slightly different using the easily available vodka and then sweetened with port wine as well as sugar.

Ingredients
2 bottles of red wine
1 bottle of port
1 cup of vodka
4 1/2 ounce sugar
1/2 bean pod vanilla
1 teaspoon whole cloves
1/2 a stick cinnamon
1/2 teaspoon ground cardamom
3 oz raisins
8 teaspoons blanched, slivered almonds

Method

1. Blend the spices, sugar, raisins and vodka and let it stand overnight.
2. Sieve before adding the red wine and the port wine.
3. Heat and serve in glass mugs to which a teaspoon of blanched, slivered almonds has been added.

Serves 8

ULLA TROUGHTON

The kilt has replaced the black cape as our current pied piper, Wes Kinghorn, leads the faithful around the cold streets bearing a lantern. Some years we have been accompanied by a brass trio, which certainly improved our pitch. We have been invited to serenade the residents of Queens Village for Seniors and enjoy stepping out of the cold into their welcoming lobby. A few home owners have opened their doors to step out on the porch and smile at our efforts. One is fondly remembered for actually inviting us in.

Banana Cake

The carollers were welcomed for many years at the Dufferin Street home of Mr. and Mrs. Clarence Peterson. We would crowd into their gracious living room, boots and all, sing our hosts a few carols and enjoy plates of chocolates and baked goods.

This recipe is a good comfort dessert which was often served to Jim, David and Tim - Mr. and Mrs. Clarence Peterson's three sons - especially when they were feeling a little under the weather.

Ingredients

1 cup white sugar
1/2 cup butter, melted
1 egg
2 tablespoons sweet milk
1 cup mashed bananas (approximately 3 bananas)
1-1/2 cups flour
1 teaspoon baking soda
1 teaspoon vanilla
1/2 teaspoon cinnamon

Method

1. Preheat oven to 375F
2. Blend the above ingredients in the order mentioned.
3. Bake in a 9″ square tin in moderate oven (375 F) for 30 minutes.

Mrs. Clarence Peterson

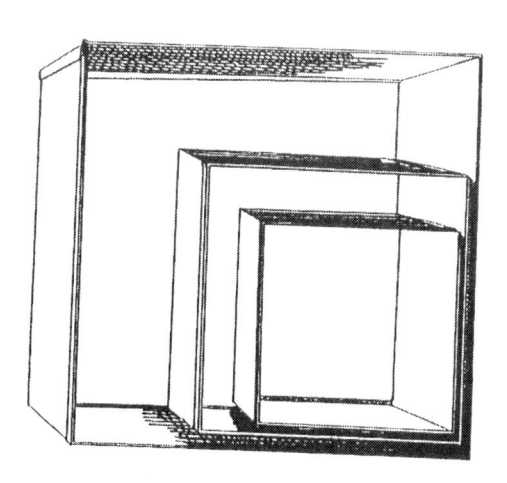

Christmas Confections

By the time our noses are blue, the bright lights decorating the McDowell home are a welcome sight. Rod is noted for his Crantinis and Joey has helped to gather a generous spread for the carollers.

The youngsters look forward to customary festive desserts. Plates of chocolate brownies, trays of decorated cookies, and always, a special toffee treat from Santa. Perhaps you could make a variation of our holiday tradition with your children.

Candied Christmas Tree

Ingredients
1/4 cup butter
1/4 cup golden syrup
1 cup granulated sugar
1 teaspoon vanilla
1 cup mixed nuts
1 cup glazed red and green cherries
1 cup glazed pineapple
1 cup dried cranberries
1 cup carmel corn

Method
1. In a large heavy skillet, melt together butter, syrup and sugar. Add vanilla.
2. Add nuts and cook, stirring, over medium-high heat for 10 to 15 minutes or until nuts are caramel coloured.
3. Draw the basic outline of a Christmas tree on a one foot piece of parchment paper on top of a backing sheet of foil.
4. Quickly spread nut mixture evenly within the tree pattern.
5. While still warm, decorate the tree with a garnish selection which has been cut to size and arranged in advance. You only have about 4 minutes to decorate this fast-setting tree.

6. Press cherries onto the ends of the branches.
7. Thin spears of pineapple can represent lights.
8. Swag popcorn and cranberry garlands across.
9. Let cool completely, peel off paper and foil. Place tree on a tray.
10. You will need a version of the Blue Bird Toffee's metal mallet to smash this tree.

SANTA'S ELVES

Chocolate Macaroons

This was a favourite treat my mother made for our birthday parties as little kids. I have no idea where the recipe originated except that Auntie Peggy (mum's friend) gave it to her. In our family they are great favourites not only for birthdays but Christmas too.

Ingredients

4 oz (one half cup) golden syrup
1-1/2 oz margarine
1 tablespoon cocoa
3 oz cornflakes (about 3 cups)
1 teaspoon vanilla essence

Method

1. Melt the first three ingredients over a gentle heat. Remove from heat.
2. Add vanilla essence.
3. Add the cornflakes. Make sure all cornflakes are well coated with the chocolate mixture.
4. Put the mixture into small paper cases in a muffin tin. Work quickly using two spoons if necessary so that the mixture does not harden in the bowl.

Julia MacGregor

The above recipe comes from Julia MacGregor's memories of her childhood. Julia is a cellist with Stratford Festival, Orchestra London and London Concert Players. She teaches cello students up to and including diploma level, at her home here in Woodfield, where friends gather around the piano at the holidays.

Traditionally, the term "Macaroons" suggests coconut. So we are giving you another version for your parties. Serve both, as one is darker than the other.

4 oz (one half cup) golden syrup
1-1/2 oz coconut oil
2 tablespoons cocoa
1 teaspoon vanilla essence
1/2 cup of desiccated coconut
2-1/2 cups of cornflakes

Mincemeat Fruitcake

Four years ago Kim Harrison renovated an old coach-house on Maitland Street between Queens Avenue and Dufferin and he has been working there ever since, holding oil painting classes as well as producing his own work.

Kim quotes French Impressionist, Pierre Bonnard saying "Large paintings are like monsters, you have to feed them everyday." A lot of work but artistically rewarding. Not so much work but gastronomically very rewarding is Kim's recipe for Mincemeat Fruitcake. A former landlady made the cake some years ago and he liked it so much she gave him the recipe. Kim says, "It appears to be a 'Christmas cake' but I make it all year round and it was a hit when served at the Annual London Artists Studio Tour."

Ingredients

2 cups prepared mincemeat – there's a type without suet if preferred.
2 cups mixed Christmas fruit (e.g. sultanas, currants, raisins, apricots, cranberries)
1 cup chopped pecans or walnuts
2-1/2 cups all purpose flour
1/2 teaspoon baking powder
1/2 teaspoon baking soda
1/4 teaspoon salt
1/4 cup butter
3/4 cup packed brown sugar
1 teaspoon vanilla
3 eggs

Method

1. Preheat oven to 325F.
2. Grease and flour a 10 inch fluted tube or bundt pan.
3. Combine mincemeat, fruit and nuts.
4. Separately combine flour, baking powder, baking soda and salt.
5. In a large bowl or electric mixer beat butter until light then add sugar, vanilla and eggs. Beat until very light and fluffy.
6. Stir in dry ingredients (batter will be stiff) and stir in fruits.
7. Bake in preheated oven for 65 minutes or until cake tests done. Cool and remove carefully from pan.

The cake can be wrapped in brandy-soaked cheesecloth if desired and overwrapped with foil. Store in a cool, dry place for at least a week before cutting.

Note: The tester could not manage to keep away from it that long.

Kim Harrison

Christmas Morning

This is generally a private time, when families circle around the tree opening presents. It is an indication of our pleasure in community gatherings that many of us forsake the joys of home and hearth to walk through the snow to Hilary and Burton Moon's home. Joan and Trevor Smith started this tradition over twenty years ago, enticing us with brandy snaps. Hilary's table is resplendent with a wheel of Stilton, sherry and biscuits. Extended families, including out-of-town members, are welcomed every year and we have checked the progress of a generation from childhood to manhood. Freshly popped corn in big bowls keeps the children nibbling. Burton and Jonathan serve hot spiced cider.

Hot Spiced Cider

At my parents' home in England, Boxing Day was always celebrated with a midmorning 'Drinks Party'. Actually the only drink that was served was Hot Mulled Hard Cider, that's fresh apple cider allowed to ferment to a certain alcohol content, a deceptively potent drink.

During the Christmas season, there was always a full wheel of Stilton Cheese on the sideboard, served only after a dinner, when the guests were sitting down and able to focus their attention on the good, subtle flavours that a Stilton renders, served at room temperature, with a glass of quality sherry or port.

Here in London, we have continued this tradition on Christmas morning. At 11.00 am, after Santa Claus has left, after all the wrapping paper has been tidily tucked away, and before the Christmas dinner is put into the oven, family and friends tumble into our tiny hallway, all muffled up against the snow, 'Ooh-ing' at the welcoming smell of hot spiced cider.

We do serve a round of Stilton Cheese , and we fortify our innocent Canadian cider, sometimes with sherry, or brandy, but in recent years, in deference to France, a country we love, we add Calvados, an Apple Brandy from Normandy.

Equipment
a large stock pot, preferably enamelled or stainless steel
a muslin-lined sieve to strain the hot cider

Ingredients
2 x 4 litre jugs of real apple cider, not apple juice (see supplier list)
1 2″ stick of cinnamon
8 whole cloves
2 2″ pieces of fresh, peeled ginger
2 fresh lemons sliced horizontally into 1/4″ thick slices
2 fresh oranges sliced horizontally into 1/4″ thick slices

Method
1. Heat all these ingredients to an upbeat simmer (do not allow to boil).
2. Simmer for about 1 hour with a lid on the pot to prevent evaporation.

I usually do this about 3 or 4 days ahead of time and just heat it up gently before guests arrive - it simplifies the occasion for me - and the spices and fruit have time to really impart their flavours to the cider.

Just before serving, I pour the hot cider through a muslin-lined sieve to strain all the pieces of apple and the spices and citrus fruits out of the cider - fruit looks very pretty in the mug, but is cumbersome to drink through.

The quality of apple cider seems to vary from jug to jug . If it seems to be rather thin in flavour, then add about 4 or 5 teabags to the hot cider, and simmer, tasting it frequently, allowing the tea to deepen and fill out the flavour - it adds an exotic tone to the punch, but make sure to take the bags out after about 15 minutes, or the bitterness of tannin will spoil the cider. This was my father's secret ingredient when he made his special Boxing Day Hot Cider !

You may also want to add a spoonful of honey if you like it a little sweeter, but don't make it so sweet that it becomes cloying.

HILARY MOON

Roast Goose

This dish is traditionally served in Denmark for Christmas Dinner, but recipes vary from family to family. These days geese have become very expensive in Denmark, so many people are now serving duck or roasted pork on Christmas Eve, however the trimmings are often the same.

At my house we served goose for years, but as the family grew and we ended up having to cook two geese, we turned to the Canadian tradition of turkey. But we still think fondly of the many Christmases, where the goose was presented before carving, decorated with Danish flags and white paper cuffs.

Ingredients
1 goose approximately 12-14 lbs.
salt and pepper

Filling:
2 cups of peeled, cored and coarsely chopped apples,
2 cups of dried prunes, pre-soaked (soak overnight) pitted and chopped,
1 large onion, peeled and quartered.

Method
1. Preheat oven to 375F.
2. Mix the ingredients for the filling and set aside
3. Empty the goose (keep the giblets) and rinse it under cold running water.
4. Pat it dry and stuff the cavity with the apple and prune filling.
5. Rub it with salt and pepper, and close the opening by lacing it with skewers and fasten the neck skin to the back of the goose.
6. Roast it on a rack set in a open roasting pan at 375 F for 3 hours.
7. As the goose fat accumulates in the pan, draw it off with a bulb baster and discard.

8. The last 1/2 hour turn the oven to 400-425 F, so the goose will be crisp and turn a beautiful brown colour.
9. Set the finished goose on a carving board, and let it sit for about 10 minutes. Then remove the skewers and scoop out the stuffing and discard it. The fruits and onion will have given flavour to the goose, but it is full of fat and therefore not too good to serve.

In Denmark we serve the goose with roasted potatoes, caramelized potatoes, sweet and sour red cabbage and gravy made in the following way:

Gravy Ingredients
goose giblets (heart, liver, neck and gizzard)
chicken bouillon
cornstarch
white wine
whipping cream
salt
pepper
browning, (optional)

Method
1. Put the giblets into a saucepan and cover it with water.
2. Add 1/2 cup of chicken bouillon to give it flavour.
3. Simmer for 1/2 hour, then sieve the stock and discard the giblets.
4. Return the stock to a saucepan and bring it to a boil.
5. Thicken with cornstarch (diluted in a bit of the stock).
6. Add some whipping cream, white wine, salt and pepper to taste.
7. A few drops of browning will give it a pleasant brown colour. (if you wish)
8. Pour the gravy into a sauce boat and serve.

Caramelized Potatoes

In Denmark this kind of potato dish is traditionally served with duck or goose on Christmas Eve.

Ingredients

2-1/2 lb small, firm potatoes
1-1/2 oz sugar
1-1/2 oz of melted butter
1 tablespoon water

Method

1. Boil the unpeeled potatoes until just done.
2. When they are cold peel them and brown them in the following manner.
3. In a Teflon coated frying pan melt the sugar until it is golden and bubbly stirring it constantly with a wooden spoon. It burns easily so watch out.
4. Then mix in the melted butter and water.
5. Add the potatoes to the caramel and keep turning them by shaking the pan until they are evenly covered and shiny.

Serves 4

Ulla Troughton

Christmas Mincemeat

Mincemeat tarts are always on the family table for Christmas dessert along with the traditional pudding. I prefer the original fruit mixture that I grew up with in England to the commercially available jars of mincemeat which seem, to me, to have a lot of filler. This traditional English recipe comes from my first cookbook over fifty years ago. It is easy to make and freezes very well. Some people might question the suet but, really, you eat so little at a time that I personally don't think it's a problem. The addition of raspberry jam nicely enhances the flavour.

Ingredients
2 lb peeled cooking apples (Granny Smith or Spy)
1 lb raisins (mixture of golden and Thompson)
1 lb sultanas
1 lb currants
3/4 lb mixed peel (or mixture peel and almonds)
1 lb suet (fine suet available in supermarkets)
1 lb sugar (I use white)
grated rind of 2 lemons
juice of 3 lemons
1 nutmeg grated
3/4 lb raspberry jam (optional)
brandy or whisky

Method
1. Wash the peeled apples and cut them into chunks.
2. Put all the dried fruit and apples in food processor and chop finer, or chop by hand, the texture will be a little different. Reserve some whole currants.
3. Transfer to large mixing bowl and stir in the sugar, suet, grated lemon rind and juice, the nutmeg and the jam if used.
4. Sprinkle in the whole currants and if possible some brandy or

whisky to make it fairly wet.
5. Mix thoroughly and put into containers in fridge.

This makes about 8 lbs of mincemeat.

To make tarts line tart tins with pastry of your choice – I use recipe on p. 175. If making ahead cover with foil and freeze and bake on the day at 400F for about 15 minutes or until lightly coloured.

If you are overwhelmed by the amount this recipe makes you can halve or quarter the amount, making sure to do that with all the ingredients.

HAZEL DESBARATS

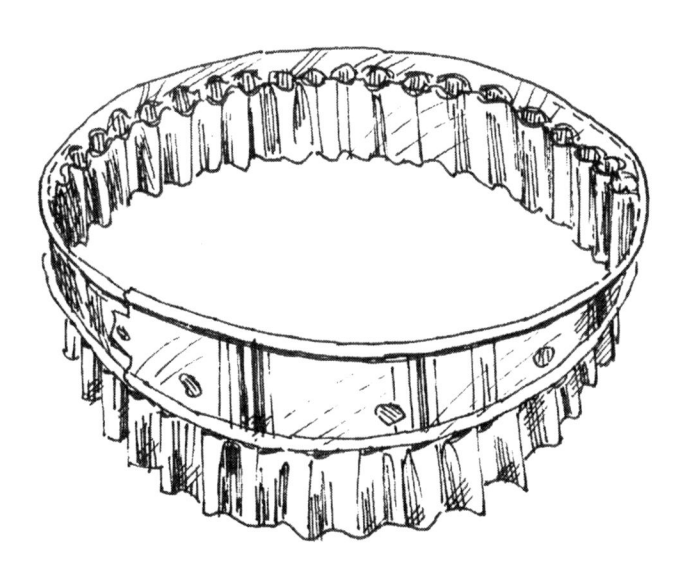

Scottish Celebrations in the New Year

On Hogmanay, New Year's Eve in Scotland, the first person to cross your threshold is called a first footer. He should bring a lump of coal to symbolize that your fire will stay lit all year. The table traditionally is set with shortbreads and whiskey to offer the visitor.

Shortbread with Whiskey

I have become smitten with the food, the music and the culture of Scotland. The bond was heightened when I visited the small community called Kinghorn. I proudly don a kilt for feast days and holidays and sometimes just for sheer pleasure.

This recipe is simple and easy, but I love it. Every year in Woodfield we host a small Burns night, for twelve or thirteen friends, and I always make shortbread. Starting from the simple base ingredients of all shortbread, I have tweaked and twisted it to my taste, blending ideas from various recipes. Most importantly, I have added Scotch. I include here a variant that reminds me a bit of Scottish Marmalade, and blends nicely with a good Speyside. Make this recipe with or without the orange and spice, sit back in a big chair with a large dram and enjoy!

Ingredients

1/2 cup of superfine sugar
1 cup soft butter
1-3/4 cups all purpose flour
1/2 cup rice flour
2 tablespoons of Single Malt Scotch
For optional 'Scottish Marmalade Style' add:
3 teaspoons fresh grated orange peel
1/4 teaspoon gound ginger
1/4 teaspoon ground cinnamon
1/8 teaspoon ground nutmeg

Method

1. Set your oven to 300 F.
2. Blend together the all purpose flour and rice flour and set aside.
3. If doing the marmalade option, blend the sugar and all spices together and set aside.
4. Spread the butter around the bottom of the bowl with a wooden

spoon
5. Sprinkle in half of the sugar (or optional sugar/spice mix) and cream into butter.
6. Beat until fairly fluffy adding sugar (or mix) as you go (add optional orange peel now).
7. Beat in the Scotch, a bit at a time so that it doesn't splash out.
8. Gradually beat in the flour mixture, a bit at a time.
9. Beat until thoroughly mixed and quite difficult to turn.
10. Knead the dough in the bowl, and roll it around the bowl to form a ball which should crack (if not, add a bit more flour).
11. Put the ball in the fridge for 45 minutes.
12. Flour (lightly) your working area, and roll out the dough to about 1/4 inch or so.
13. Cut into shapes. I use a 3.5˝ cutter shaped as a Westie (our West Highland White Terrier).
14. Arrange them onto a baking sheet, lined with parchment paper.
15. Bake for 30 minutes or until the edges are just turning golden (more or less to your taste).
16. Remove from the oven, and after a few minutes on the sheet to firm up, cool them on a rack.

This recipe will make from 15 to 30 cookies depending on your cutter size and shape.

WES KINGHORN

New Year's Levée

Lorraine de Blois and Michael Robbins invite friends to a warming Quebecois buffet on New Year's Day: flowers, music, fires roaring and wine pouring. Michael stations himself at one end of the large kitchen island, shucking fresh oysters and pouring mimosas. Lorraine has set a long table with:

terrine of rabbit paté
wheatberry salad (see page 45)
grated carrot salad with raisins and pecans
a whole round of brie with fig chutney
asparagus spears with smoked salmon
radicchio with capers, horseradish, boiled eggs, endive

But guests head first for the bubbling pot of black bean "cassoulet" soup, Silver Palate's popular take on a south of France classic. A bowlful, topped with a spoon of sour cream, welcomes a new year on a snowy afternoon.

Resolutions for a New Year in the Kitchen

Twelfth Night Cassoulet

In the 1970's, when Ginette Bisaillon owned the Auberge du Petit Prince, she observed the rituals of Twelfth Night, the Eve of the Epiphany. January sixth, the twelfth day after Christmas, became marked by revelry and reversal of roles. Whoever found the coin in the cake was crowned King for the Night. One year, the dish washer, Chris Squire got to wear the paper crown, then prophetically assumed Ginette's mantle several years later. Everyone lined up along the counter in the restaurant kitchen waiting their turn to be served from the huge cast iron pot on the Garland stove. You could detect the ingredients of her cassoulet from the heady aroma - lots of garlic, thyme, duck or goose confit, pork sausages, white beans, all simmering in a rich tomato sauce. We generally roast a goose at Christmas so that we can save wings, legs and bits for the pot. In a token reversal of roles, David prepares this meal.

Equipment

This recipe takes its name from the earthenware casserole in which it was originally prepared in the Languedoc region of France. Every other store in the town of Castlenaudry has a picture of a casserole hanging from its shingle. We use a French enamelled dutch oven so that it can go from the top of the stove into the oven.

Ingredients

1-1/2 lbs. dry Great Northern or haricot beans
1 medium size onion
1 preserved duck leg (confit)
2 wings and other left-over bits from the roast goose
1 lb. coarse garlic pork sausage
3 cloves garlic
3 fresh tomatoes or 1 small can diced
2 cups beef bouillon (see supplier list)
bay leaf, thyme, salt, pepper
1 1/2 cup breadcrumbs to cover the top

Method

1. Soak beans in water overnight. Drain.
2. Place beans and a garlic clove in a large sauce pan, cover with fresh water, bring to a boil, skim foam off top and simmer until nearly tender. Don't overcook.
3. In a frying pan with a lid, simmer sausage in water until partially cooked. Drain.
4. Using the same frying pan or a sauce pan lightly sauté the sliced onion along with the sausage.
5. When the onion slices are translucent, add 2 crushed garlic cloves and the tomatoes.
6. Stir in 2 cups bouillon
7. Add bay leaf, 1/2 teaspoon of dry thyme, salt and pepper to taste to mixture in fry pan. Simmer for 15 or 20 minutes.
8. Put preserved duck leg (confit) along with cut up sausage pieces and goose bits into the bottom of a large bean pot or cast iron casserole.
9. Cover with the drained beans (do not save the bean liquid)
10. Pour over the stock/frying pan mixture.
11. Preheat oven to 350F
12. Cover and bake in a 350F degree oven for an hour and a half. For the last half hour or so of baking, remove the lid and cover the beans with bread crumbs to finish cooking. The dish is finished when the liquid has mostly been absorbed and a crust has formed

on top.

Serves 6 to 8 people. A French baguette and young red wine goes well with this dish.

David Lindsay

The twelfth day after Christmas represents the end of the festive season. Decorations are packed away. Dead trees are dragged to the boulevard for pick-up. As the snow transforms Woodfield into a scene from Currier and Ives, our President, Wes, fortified by his wee dram, experiments with his new snow blower by clearing six neighbouring driveways. The rest of us huddle by the fireplace, leafing through garden catalogues, dreaming of spring.

A HEALTHY FUTURE

Towards a Healthy Future

Melissa Briones and Kristen Gaudet live next door to each other on Prospect Avenue. Melissa is a registered consulting dietitian. Kristen is also a registered dietitian and the very busy mother of three young children.

They volunteered to put on their professional hats for this final chapter to help us towards a healthy future. They can explain it best in their own words.

As we look back on our childhood memories, we realize how food has played such a huge role in shaping our professional and personal lives. Whether we cooked with our parents, participated in baking activities, washed vegetables from the backyard garden or tasted a variety of raw vegetables, food fostered feelings of warmth and comfort. Although life has gotten busier and we are no longer able to spend a lot of time preparing our meals, we need to continue to make it a priority to appreciate and enjoy the wonderful experience of food everyday.

We are excited to share this food culture with you. We feel that it is essential that we try to reconnect with the concept of eating for nourishment, rather than for convenience, and to create a healthy and sustainable future for our community. This could be as simple as having a garden, shopping at farmers' markets for local, fresh produce and limiting processed foods. Choosing whole foods will not only reduce the amount of additives but also provide you with optimal nutrient intake and better control over what you are consuming.

In this chapter, we hope to provide you with some ideas and inspirations to cook healthy and naturally. We want to promote eating healthy as delicious, smart, practical and sustainable in order to foster the pleasures of our food for today and for our future generation.

Bon appetit!
MELISSA BRIONES MH Sc REGISTERED DIETITIAN
KRISTEN GAUDET BSc REGISTERED DIETITIAN

Homemade Granola

Granola is a good source of iron and whole grains but store bought options can also be rich in saturated and trans fats and additives. Try this easy homemade recipe as a great source of a variety of healthy unsaturated fats, fibre and protein made only from all natural ingredients. I serve this to my family as a staple food item that can be eaten as a cereal with fruit on top or added to yogurt as a snack.

Equipment
You will need two of your largest baking or roasting pans, about 18" by 13" by 2". The grains and seeds need to be spread out no more than 1/2" deep in order to bake evenly.

Ingredients
5 cups of rolled oats (large flakes)
1/2 cup oat or wheat bran
1/4 cup pumpkin seeds (raw)
1/2 cup sunflower seeds (preferably unsalted)
1/2 cup almonds, sliced
1/2 cup chopped pecans or walnuts
1/4 cup flax seeds (optional)
1 cup large-flake coconut
1/2 cup raisins, dried cranberries or other dried fruit
1/2 cup sunflower oil
1/2 cup pure maple syrup
1-2 teaspoon cinnamon (optional)
4 tablespoons barley malt syrup or honey
2 teaspoons vanilla extract

Method
1. Preheat oven to 350 F.
2. Lightly oil pan.

3. Combine all dry ingredients together in a large bowl.
4. Reserve fruits - raisins, cranberries to add when granola is finished baking.
5. Mix the sunflower oil, maple syrup and barley malt in a separate bowl.
6. Add extract and pour the maple mixture into the large bowl of dry ingredients.
7. Stir well to completely coat the dry ingredients.
8. Spread the granola on the baking pans. Bake for about 30 minutes, until golden. Stir about every ten minutes to guarantee even browning. You may want to do these in separate batches depending on the size and air circulation in your oven. Watch to prevent scorching.
9. Stir in a selection of fruits of your choice when mixture is cooled.
10. Store in airtight jars for no longer than a month.

KRISTEN GAUDET

Banana Pancakes

A low fat, healthy breakfast item for all to enjoy. I used to love these as an afternoon snack when I was a kid. You can double this recipe and freeze extra pancakes as a snack on another day. Feel free to add your choice of fruit such as berries and top with maple syrup. This recipe is preferable to pre-made mixes.

Equipment
A cast iron frying pan or flat griddle. A coated pan would work if it is not light weight. Pancakes can scorch easily.

Ingredients
3/4 cup each of whole wheat flour and all purpose flour
1-1/2 tablespoons sugar
1 teaspoon baking powder
1 teaspoon baking soda
2 egg whites
1-1/2 cups buttermilk
1/4 cup 1% cottage cheese
1/2 teaspoon pure vanilla
2 mashed bananas
canola or grapeseed oil

Method
1. In a large bowl, combine dry ingredients.
2. In a smaller bowl, combine egg whites, buttermilk, cottage cheese, vanilla and mashed bananas.
3. Add buttermilk mixture to the dry ingredients and stir until dry ingredients are moistened. Do not over stir as the pancakes will not rise.
4. Heat a cast iron frying pan or flat griddle with a surface coating of grapeseed oil.

5. Ladle on about 1/2 cup of batter for each pancake.
6. Flip over pancakes when you see bubbles forming on top.

Makes about 8 large pancakes.

KRISTEN GAUDET

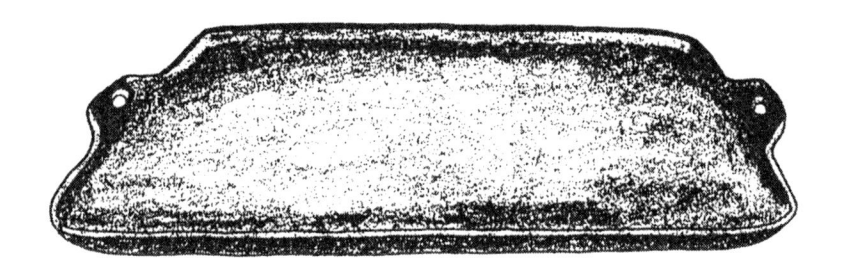

Alicia's Maple Smoothie

Alicia Wilkin's favourite smoothie combination inspired us to present other alternatives for fast, nutritious breakfasts and afternoon energy boosts. Homemade smoothies are an excellent way to pack a lot of nutrition and give an ultimate energy boost without any unpleasant surprises or hidden quantities of saturated fats or refined sugars. When choosing fresh fruits, look for rich colours such as red, purple and blue. Always choose very fragrant fruits as they have a more developed, fuller flavour. Frozen fruits are also ideal for smoothies as they have not lost many nutrients from the freezing process and are available during the winter season.

Children love the taste of smoothies in the morning and it is a great way for parents to sneak in some vitamins, minerals, and probiotics.

Ingredients
1-1/4 cup strawberries
3/4 cup blueberry yogurt (0% fat works)
1/2 cup milk
2 tablespoons maple syrup.

Method
Blend all ingredients with a hand held blender until smooth.

Makes about 2 cups.

Alicia Wilkins

Additional Smoothie Combinations

Our favourite is a sliced banana whirled with plain yogurt and orange/mango juice.

Suggested fruits: blackberries, raspberries, blueberries, bananas, kiwi, peach slices.

Try these juice flavours: cranberry, orange, mango, pear, pineapple

Other sweeteners: honey, corn syrup

Creamy liquids: soy milk, rice drink, almond milk, tofu, flavoured yogurts, kefir, buttermilk, or a combination with cottage cheese.

Add fibre! In addition to the fibre provided by the fresh fruits used, you can also add a tablespoon of ground seed (i.e. flax) or crushed bran.

Add healthy fats! Avocados are a great source of unsaturated fats and fat soluble vitamins.

Add protein! In addition to the dairy products used in this recipe, sliced almonds (or other nuts or seeds) are great ways to add a little crunch and increase protein to the mix. Protein will help to increase satiety and reduce hunger.

Melissa Briones
Kristen Gaudet

Health Smart Lunch

Lunch could very well be the most challenging meal to co-ordinate for you and your family. While some may have the opportunity to be at home for lunch, many must have some foresight to bring a healthy lunch to work or school.

In order to have the option of preparing my lunch in 10 minutes or less (whether it is the night before, or the morning), I always keep some key ingredients from each food group on hand. Take a moment to list which foods are favourites in your home.

Breads or Grain:
- whole grain bread or pita. The heavier the better as weight indicates the amount of whole grains and fibre contained in the product.
- couscous or pre-made quinoa

Vegetables:
- pre-made roasted red peppers (ideal for sandwiches)
- assorted pre-washed lettuces and spinach
- tomatoes
- cucumbers

Meat and Alternatives:
- tuna
- leftovers (chicken, beef, etc.)
- prepared chickpeas or kidney beans
- assortment of cheeses

With quick ingredients on hand, making a smart, simple, healthy and delicious lunch is possible to give you more time to enjoy the pleasure of eating and taking a needed midday break.

Wrap it Up (No recipe necessary)

The formula to this meal is to include the following elements:

The wrap (whole grain or corn tortilla)

A component that is:
- Wet (sauces, spreads)
- Crunchy (lettuce, celery, carrots, corn, cucumbers, apples)
- Red (peppers, tomatoes, sundried tomatoes, cranberries)
- Protein (chicken, tuna, cheese, kidney beans, etc)

Wrap up all the ingredients and savour a hearty lunch.

Melissa Briones

Andes Omelet

Never underestimate the impact of simple ideas. A child nutrition program in the Andes, that I was fortunate enough to participate in, provided the exceptional offering of a hen to each child in a school that we had determined was suffering from malnutrition. Each child was to eat two eggs a day from its chicken's output, share additional eggs with family and sell any remaining. The project returned fabulous results, with the majority of the children increasing their weight and height to within a healthy range for their age in just a year.

There are not too many foods more versatile than an egg. Eggs are a great source of protein and offer a very quick and easy way to create a meal as simple or complex in flavours as you wish.

Hardboiled, scrambled, folded, and separated. Bright, round and orange like the morning sunrise, organic and free-run eggs are certainly a treat and provide a delectable breakfast, brunch or lunch.

Ingredients

2 eggs equal one protein portion (I find one egg is enough for me)
milk – just a splash
your choice of vegetables - green or red peppers, onions, mushrooms, sundried tomatoes, fresh tomatoes, spinach, kale, swiss chard, eggplant, leeks, green onions
cheese (optional) - goat cheese, cottage, feta.
fresh herbs (a great alternative to salt) – cilantro, basil, oregano
olive oil

Method

1. Heat a skillet with olive oil. A little bit of butter may be added for flavour in combination with the olive oil if preferred.
2. Sauté the vegetables until soft and set aside. Keep the pan heated.
3. Beat the eggs and milk together. Pour beaten eggs into skillet and

allow to cook until the egg protein is slightly fixed.
4. Sprinkle cheese, sautéed vegetables and fresh herbs into egg mixture and fold over.
5. Allow the egg to cook through. Flip once to ensure thorough cooking of the egg.

Serve with a slice of toast and fresh fruit to make a complete meal.

MELISSA BRIONES

Tasty Supper Tips

Supper was always an important time in the day for my family as I grew up. It was a time to relax, to nourish our bodies and our relationships, to talk about our day's accomplishments and challenges while we enjoyed a delicious variety of dishes and flavours. Trying to maintain this daily tradition can be tricky considering many long days and hectic schedules, but with a little bit of organization in the kitchen, every night can offer this experience.

The following are some kitchen tips to ensure that a healthy and complete supper is less than 30 minutes away.

- Prepare items such as pasta sauces, soups and broths ahead of time (weekend or day off). Once made, label the items and place in fridge or freezer.
- Clean all vegetables and fruits when you buy them so that they are ready to use when you need them.
- Make enough for leftovers (i.e. if you are baking chicken, make enough for sandwiches the next day)
- Keep your spice rack and flavourings well stocked and fresh to add variety to all your meals
  Asian: sesame seed/oil, soya sauce, fish sauce, ginger, green onions
  Indian: cumin, curry, coriander seed, chilies
  Italian: oregano, basil, tomatoes, garlic
  Latin American: lime, chilies, chipotle, cilantro
  comforting herbs: rosemary, thyme, sage
- Vegetables: Steaming or roasting are heart healthy preparation methods which also reduce the amount of nutrients lost in the cooking process.
- Keep colour in mind when choosing vegetables, make sure your fridge is vibrant with red, purple, green (dark and light), white, yellow and orange

- Meat and Alternatives: Choose lean meats often and when possible remove the skin from poultry items; marbled meats have more fat and should be used less frequently. Tofu is a good option.
- Offer whole grain and brown rice instead of white because of the higher fibre and iron content.

Remember that supper is simple. The ideal plate should be 1/2 vegetables, 1/4 meat or alternatives and 1/4 grains/starch.

MELISSA BRIONES

Simple Snacks

Having healthy snacks available such as sliced fruits, raisins or dates, almonds or other nuts, yogurt, cheese with healthy crackers, veggies and low fat dips, will reduce the temptation to snack on higher fat convenient items (ie. potato chips, chocolate bar, cookies, pop). Fruits cleaned and placed in a visible area will increase the possibility of them being eaten.

Fresh Salsa – An Anytime Food!

I will never forget the first time I ever had fresh salsa. I was storm-stayed in a dodgy cantina in Cozumel, Mexico with nothing to do but have a cerveza. When the waiter brought a bowl of coarsely diced vegetables and some fresh corn chips, in an instant, my world changed. I suddenly realized that salsa was not just a bright red mash of tomatoes in a jar, but rather, it can be as fresh and wholesome as a salad. Although I have yet to figure out how to re-create the exact salsa I ate that day, I do continue to enjoy the simple basics of the dish.

Ingredients
1 lb tomatoes, diced
1 red onion, diced
2 cloves garlic (or more if preferred), minced
1 bunch cilantro, chopped
2 chilies (these can be as hot or as mild as you like), finely diced
1 lime
salt and pepper

Optional vegetables: adobo chilies, bell peppers, green onions.
Fruits such as mangoes, papayas or pineapples are also great variations.

Optional spices: ground cumin, coriander, cayenne.

Please remember that these ingredients can be readily grown in a "salsa garden" in the summer.

Method

1. Combine all ingredients in a bowl and season with salt and pepper.
2. Juice the lime into the mix for additional vitamin C and to preserve the colours.

This simple salsa can be used in an omelet at breakfast; as a condiment for quesadillas or wraps for lunch, served on top of baked or grilled chicken or fish for supper or used in place of regular pizza sauce. Also delicious served with corn tortillas.

Melissa Briones

Carrot Yogurt Dip

This is a recipe from my Turkish friend Hitay Yukseker. It offers a healthy alternative to packaged dips that are loaded with salts, fats, cheeses and stale seasonings.

Ingredients

1 pound of carrots
1 to 1 1/2 cups of yogurt, 6% fat, Balkan style (less yogurt gives more flavour)
1 to 4 cloves of garlic
1 teaspoon oil
pinch of salt

Method

1. Scrub then steam whole carrots.
2. Peel carrots and cut into chunks.
3. Blend all ingredients in the food processor.

Serve with pita chips or celery sticks.

Regina Moorcroft

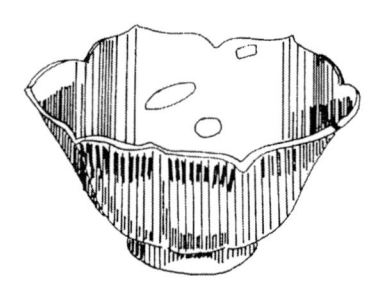

Squash-Cheese Dip

For every meal or snack, I aim for at least 3 out of the 4 food groups to ensure variety and nutrition. My children love cheese and I am pleased about the added vegetables. It calls for either sweet potato or butternut squash purée. Rich in beta carotene and potassium, they are great for keeping both skin and eyes healthy and contribute to heart health.

Ingredients

1/2 cup grated cheese
1 cup sweet potato or butternut squash purée (can be made ahead of time and stored in the freezer in plastic bags)
1-1/2 teaspoon butter
1/4 teaspoon salt (optional)
2 slices of whole wheat or multigrain bread
carrot and celery sticks and other raw vegetables of choice

Method

1. Preheat oven to 400F.
2. Bake squash halves, flesh down for 45 minutes at 400F. Scoop out flesh and purée in food processor.
3. If using, peel sweet potatoes. Boil or steam until tender.
4. Blend in a food processor or use a hand masher, until creamy smooth.
5. Mix grated cheese, vegetable purée, butter and salt.
6. Warm in the oven in an open small casserole until cheese is melted.
7. Set warm dipping dish in the centre of a large platter surrounded by toasted whole wheat bread squares, carrot, celery sticks, and broccoli spears.

Kristen Gaudet

Banana Chocolate Chip Muffins

This recipe comes from my grandmother's collection. These are great for breakfast and/or a snack. They are low fat and nutritious. Of course the chocolate chips are a huge hit with my kids. I usually double or triple this recipe so I can freeze extra muffins.

Ingredients

1 cup of quick rolled oats
1/2 cup all purpose flour
1/2 cup whole wheat flour
1/4 cup wheat germ (keep refrigerated)
1/4 cup sugar
1-1/2 teaspoons baking powder
1 teaspoon baking soda
1/2 teaspoon sea salt
3 large mashed bananas (ripe)
2 egg whites
1/4 cup melted butter
1/2 cup chocolate chips

Method

1. Preheat oven to 375 F.
2. Combine all dry ingredients in a large bowl.
3. In a small bowl, mix mashed bananas, butter and egg whites.
4. Then add to dry mixture and mix until just moistened. (Do not overmix as the muffins will become tough and rubbery).
5. Stir in chocolate chips.
6. Add to oiled muffin tins and bake for approximately 15 to 20 minutes (or until toothpick inserted in center comes out clean).

Makes about 12 muffins.

Kristen Gaudet

Cooking at Lord Roberts

Nan Finlayson introduced cooking to hundreds of Woodfield children in the twenty years she was kindergarden teacher at Lord Roberts French Immersion School. As you will see when you read her recipes, created in the classroom with her eager pupils, important life skills accompanied the cooking techniques. It would be interesting to find out how many of her graduates now reside as adults, with kitchens of their own, in our community.

Bleak House, which once stood on the site of the school, no doubt had an apple tree in the garden, from which Mrs. Macbeth would have made applesauce for the ailing Col. Talbot. The children brought some history back to life when they made La Compote de Pommes in the classroom. We are including Nan's explanation of the lesson in her own words in case parents would like to use her method to encourage their children in the kitchen.

"This was an all day Friday activity at the end of October to celebrate our first two months of school. The activity involved -"

1. A math lesson - sorting out apples by size, shape, colour, stems/no stems, shiny/not shiny, and counting each pile.
2. A French language lesson- grand, petit, moyen, rouge, vert, jaune.
3. An English language lesson - How do apples look? What do you think they will look like later when cooked? Describe their smell.
4. A health lesson - always wash hands before we start. Show them the safest way to cut an apple into little pieces. Explain that we are using healthy produce.
5. Environmental lesson - use locally grown produce that supports litterless lunches
6. Art lesson - cut the apple in half horizontally to see the star. Used for later projects.

7. Science lesson - heat conductivity - Why do we use a wooden spoon? Why are there black handles on the pan and lid? Why do we add water? Why do we put the lid on the pan when the apples are cooking?

Now we are ready to start cooking.

La Compote de Pommes

Equipment
saucepan, wooden spoon, bowl, ladle,
moulin legumes (food mill)
knives (dull butter knives were used with the children)

Ingredients
each child was asked to bring in an apple
brown sugar to taste
cinnamon

Method

1. Cut apples into small pieces, stems, cores, skins, and all.
2. Place apple pieces in saucepan. Add water to two thirds the height of the apples.
3. Cook over low heat until apples are soft.
4. Ladle into the food mill.
5. Grind through the sieve into a large bowl. Each child had a chance to turn the handle of the moulin.
6. Stir in brown sugar to taste.
7. Spoon into serving bowls and sprinkle with cinnamon.

Seconds quelque un?

We would read many apple books and sing lots of apple songs. La belle pomme. C'est l'automne!!

Cranberry Relish

This is an activity we enjoyed when discussing family traditions during the month of December. The students especially enjoyed watching and listening to the orange sections and the whole cranberries move through the old-fashioned meat grinder to come out all ground up.

"Oh look, there's a piece of orange!"

"Oh, listen to the cranberries pop!"

Equipment

a meat grinder (it was my mother's - an activity that I loved to watch as a child and in which my own children participated)
bowl, spoon, small jelly jars

Ingredients

1 bag of fresh cranberries
1 orange
white sugar

Method

1. Each child would put a few cranberries and a small section of orange through the grinder.
2. Add sugar and let children taste to achieve correct amount.
3. The remaining mixture we would spoon into small jars, add a colourful material cover, and deliver to the caretaker, secretary, librarian, principal, gym teacher, as a small token of our thanks for their contribution to our well-being.

Merci

Sushi Sandwiches

At the end of February we celebrated the end of two months of activities centered around the theme of me and my family, "Moi et ma famille", when we studied our families, healthy foods, healthy emotions, healthy ways of expressing those emotions, community helpers, and the importance of being good caretakers of our community (animals as well as humankind).

Parents were invited to our classroom to see our artwork, books and resident pet "Patch".

They were invited to join us in song and dance. We served sushi sandwiches which we had made earlier that morning. Bon appetit.

Equipment
rolling pin
spreading knife
basket lined with a colourful cloth napkin

Ingredients
whole wheat bread sliced
hummus and/or cream cheese and/or soft goat cheese
matchstick slices of carrots, cucumber, celery 6 inches long
herbs from the school garden - dill, mint, parsley, chives

Method
1. Flatten the bread slices with the rolling pin
2. Spread hummus, cream cheese or goat cheese.
3. Sprinkle with herbs.
4. Lay vegetable matchsticks at the bottom end of each slice. Let a little hang over the edge.
5. Roll up bread slice pressing gently to seal.
6. Slice into three equal parts and place in basket to serve.

Is it any wonder Nan's daughter Ellen, is now a chef in a restaurant? And her daughter Meg is a very creative cook. Her son is a long-distance runner.

Local Suppliers

Woodfield residents can walk or bicycle to many independent retailers. Local sources offer some of the best produce in the city. Since the 1830's, a central market has been in the city's core.

1. *Covent Garden Market 130 King Street 519-439-3921*
    Open 7 days a week. Outdoor farmers' market on Thursday and Saturday mornings May through December.

Doris Family Produce carries a line of bouillon paste in jars called, "Better than Bouillon." It is available in chicken, beef, mushroom, vegetable and lobster flavours. Just one teaspoon to a cup of boiling water for a tasty stock. Also check out the bottles of Aurora tomato sauce. Chris Doris has developed his own infused garlic/basil olive oil, subtly perfect for dipping a hearty bread or sprinkling on veg and salads. Watch for further products bearing the label "For the Love of."

Smith Cheese stocks an innovative selection of Canadian cheeses in addition to a gamut of imported. Glenda also offers freshly made pasta and an array of olives, pitted or not.

Anna at *Kleibers' Deli* carries the Indonesian condiments required for Irene Say's recipe.

Chris Havaris can supply you with organic grains and pulses, such as quinoa, split peas and lentils. In addition to his stalls of produce, a cooler holds blocks of tofu and other bio-soya products.

Snack and Bake carries flours, sugars, dried bottles of herbs and spices. In season, you will find all of the dried fruits and nuts required to bake a holiday cake.

Field Gate Organics, a butcher shop with organic meats as well as vegetables from *Soiled Reputations*, organic dairy products and baked goods.

The outdoor vendors sell fresh trout, bison meat, and maple syrup. Rick Cornelissen of *Eco-Logic Nursery* follows the seasons from the earliest spinach and radish to gourds, beets and Christmas greenery. His bags of dried beans appear in the fall and are worth stocking up on.

Doloway Organic Gardens always has a variety of just-picked organic herbs and mesclun.

2. *Jill's Table* 115 King Street 519-645-1335
Many of our submitters referred readers to Jill's for tart tins, flan pans and other batterie de cuisine. She also carries the preferred San Marzano brand of Italian tomatoes and refrigerated goodies, such as duck confit.

3. *Sunripe Produce* 744 Adelaide Street North 519-433-4141
Rod McDowell's pasta recipes call for Pink Lady brand hot sausages and the bacon stocked in this local produce store. Many Woodfielders appreciate their carefully chosen greens and fruit.

4. *London Co-op Store* 621 Princess Avenue 519-679-0570
Now in its fortieth year, this whole foods mini-market carries organic produce, frozen meat and fish entrées, tofu, vegetarian and macrobiotic condiments, grains, and dairy products.

5. *Atlantic Sea Fish Market* 708 Hamilton Road 519-452-7511
   Centre Ocean Food 778 Hamilton Road 519-452-1220
Frequented by fresh ocean fish lovers.

6. *Far East Mart   106-25 Oxford Street West   519-643-0174*
The preserved black beans used to prepare Haiyun Chen's spare ribs can be found here in copious amounts for very little money, as can most other oriental condiments.

7. *Everspring Farms   14821 Ten Mile Road R.R. #3 Ilderton   519-659-5054*
It is worth the short country drive to visit this poultry supplier for a fresh young goose.

8. *Fadel's Variety   574 Adelaide St. N. at Elias St.   519-434-3435*
A neighbourhood stop for feta cheese, olives and a few vegetables in season.

Metric Conversion Chart

Imperial	Metric
1/4 teaspoon	1.25 millilitres
1/2 teaspoon	2.5 millilitres
1 teaspoon	5 millilitres
1 tablespoon	15 millilitres
1 fluid ounce	30 millilitres
1/4 cup	60 millilitres
1/3 cup	80 millilitres
1/2 cup	120 millilitres
1 cup	240 millilitres
2 cups	480 millilitres
4 cups (32 ounces)	960 millilitres (.96 litre)

Weights

1 ounce	28 grams
1/4 pound (4 ounces)	114 grams
1 pound (16 ounces)	454 grams
2.2 pounds	1 kilogram (1000 grams)

Oven Temperature Equivalents

Degrees Fahrenheit	Degrees Celsius
200	90
250	120
300 - 325	150 - 160
325 - 350	160 - 180
350 - 375	180 - 190
375 - 400	190 - 200
400 - 450	200 - 230
450 - 500	230 - 260

LaVergne, TN USA
23 April 2010
180229LV00005B/2/P